FEMINIST
EXPERIENCES

FEMINIST EXPERIENCES

The Women's Movement in Four Cultures

SUSAN BASSNETT

*Senior Lecturer in Comparative Literature,
University of Warwick*

London
ALLEN & UNWIN
Boston   Sydney

**Allen & Unwin (Publishers) Ltd,
40 Museum Street, London WC1A 1LU, UK**

Allen & Unwin (Publishers) Ltd,
Park Lane, Hemel Hempstead, Herts HP2 4TE, UK

Allen & Unwin, Inc.,
8 Winchester Place, Winchester, Mass. 01890, USA

Allen & Unwin (Australia) Ltd,
8 Napier Street, North Sydney, NSW 2060, Australia

First published in 1986

British Library Cataloguing in Publication Data

Bassnett, Susan
  Feminist experiences: the women's movement
  in four cultures.
  1. Feminism
  I. Title
  305.4′2   HQ1122
  ISBN 0–04–301273–6
  ISBN 0–04–301274–4 Pbk

Library of Congress Cataloging-in-Publication Data

Bassnett, Susan.
  Feminist experiences.

Bibliography: p.
Includes index.
  1. Feminism – Cross-cultural studies. 2. Feminism –
United States – History – 19th century. 3. Feminism –
Germany (East) – History – 19th century. 4. Feminism –
Italy – History – 19th century. 5. Feminism – Great
Britain – History – 19th century.   I. Title.
HQ1154.B324   1986   305.4′2   86–10908
  ISBN 0–04–301273–6 (U.S.: alk. paper)
  ISBN 0–04–301274–4 (U.S.: pbk.: alk. paper)

Set in 11 on 12 point Garamond by Nene Phototypesetters Ltd
and printed in Great Britain by Billings and Sons Ltd, London and Worcester

For my mother and my daughters

Contents

Acknowledgements

Many people have helped in the preparation and writing of this book. I owe particular thanks to Farrell Burnett, also to Vita Fortunati, Giovanna Franci and the staff of the Librellula in Bologna. My thanks also to Stefanie Liedtke from Panorama DDR, who took such pains to help me with the research in the GDR. I am grateful to Irene Pearson, who typed the manuscript, and, as ever, thanks are due to Stella Dixon and to my mother, husband and daughters Lucy and Vanessa, without whom I should not have had the time or space in which to write at all.

Introduction

The women's movement is usually referred to as if it were a constant, global phenomenon. There are women's movements in Europe, North and South America, Africa, the Middle East, India, Japan and Australia, and there is an assumption in the minds of men and women alike that the movements are regional developments of the same thing, sharing a common core. But anyone who is familiar with more than one culture soon becomes aware not so much of similarities as of differences between women's movements, of variations in emphasis, in priorities, in tactics and in aims. As someone who has no definitive roots in any one culture, I have been able to consider some of those differences in four societies without being prejudiced in favour of any one of them, and through the process of comparing I have asked myself the question whether there is any universal trans-cultural feminist thought and aspiration, or whether the demands of women in any context are conditioned by the history of men and women in that society.

I have gone back beyond the recent resurgence of feminism that has come to be termed 'the women's movement' and looked at the history of feminism in the nineteenth century. In so doing, I have had to reappraise the very term 'feminism'. Since its first appearance in the eighteenth century there have been two main lines of development – liberal feminism, of the kind that flourished in the United States, and revolutionary or socialist feminism. In examining the four societies in this book I have traced those two often conflicting lines through the stages of their development within their national contexts as part of an attempt to explain the differences in concepts of feminism today. So, for example, in Britain and the United States, the prevailing tradition has been that of liberal feminism, sometimes described in denigratory terms as bourgeois feminism, which reflects the consistency in the processes of democratic government in both countries. In Italy, on the contrary, liberal feminism has played little part in the rebirth of feminism in the late 1960s, but then Italy has undergone radical changes in the past century alone, moving from a nation of small ducalities to unification in 1870, then through a period of fascist rule, a war of occupation, a civil war and the subsequent rise in the postwar period of the largest communist party outside eastern Europe. The energy of the Italian women's movement reflects the violent changes that have swept through Italian society.

Equally, the emergence of what can be described as feminism in the German Democratic Republic (GDR) derives from the particular history of the new postwar Germany. While Western feminists wrestle with what Heidi Hartmann has called 'the unhappy marriage of Marxism and feminism'[1], women in the GDR have considered the woman question from a totally different perspective, from within socialism rather than from outside. The fundamental debate on the nature of patriarchy still goes on, but East German women are bound to see the terms of that debate very differently.

My analysis of the differences between the four societies is the basis of this book. I have focused on the violence of the Italian women's movement, on its intellectualism, on its energy. In analysing the American women's movement I have dwelt on its roots in the past and on what seem to be its inherent contradictions, due to a belief in pragmatic solutions. Discussing the GDR I have tried to show how a sense of feminism on a completely new basis is emerging through other means than those of the organized women's movements elsewhere, and have found myself looking at the problem of the relationship between Marxism and feminism with new eyes. The greatest problems have been presented by my attempts to look at the women's movement in Britain, because try as I might, I found myself continually returning not so much to problems of feminism as to problems of class. The mysteries of the British class system pervade every aspect of British life, and the women's movement is not exempt.

The writing of this book derived from an attempt to clarify for myself a series of problems and contradictions that could not easily be resolved. During what should ideally have been a process of clarification, some of those complex issues came more sharply into focus, but at the same time a whole new set of questions that I had never thought to pose also appeared and are still a long way from being satisfactorily resolved.

Underlying this book are two distinct problems. The first is one of method, for although I have attempted a comparative study of the women's movement in four societies, I am well aware that I have not structured the book as a comprehensive examination of four social contexts. Instead, I have written out of my experience of the movement in the four countries with which I am most familiar. Had I begun differently, using criteria of supposedly 'objective' scholarship, I should certainly have chosen other societies than the four in question. I should have included a section on France, for example, should have extended the German section to include the Federal Republic and should also have looked at the development of the women's movement in Australia and New Zealand. Instead, I chose to write only about those countries in which I had lived, worked, travelled and made friends, places where I feel relatively at home and able to make comments as an insider, rather than as an outsider whose perspective would be that of the neutral investigator.

The problem of finding a balance between personal experience and academic discourse is not my difficulty alone; it is central to the whole area of work known as women's studies. In the structures of Western social institutions, such as legal and educational systems, there is an assumption that objectivity can and does exist and that the personal, emotional side ought to be suppressed in the interests of that supposed objectivity. A major advance in European feminist thought over the last fifteen years has been the mounting of a challenge to that binary division, together with an invitation to both sexes to rethink the terms on which society is based. Since the eighteenth century, we have been urged to uphold the merits of rationalism, to see reason as weighing more heavily than emotion, and, significantly, to see reason as principally a male capacity and emotion as principally a female one. The fact that the reason – emotion distinction might be a fairly recent construct, since prior to what we have come to call the Age of Reason it was not so clear-cut, seems never to have been seriously challenged until today. Now it does seem possible to talk about reinstating the irrational even the anti-rational as positive virtues, and by doing this we are signalling that the age of reason and science has had its day. After all, in Shakespeare's time a mathematician could also lay claims to being a magician, and the boundaries between proof and belief were infinitely more fluid than might be acceptable today.

This book is therefore a personal perspective and a serious study of the changing patterns of feminist thought and practice in four societies. It looks at the re-emergence of feminism since the 1960s and attempts to locate these developments in a historical context, since women's movements do have their own past and have not simply sprung up inexplicably out of nowhere.

I chose to arrange my investigations of the four societies in the order that seemed to emerge from a questioning of the basis of feminism. The United States, as the place where the new feminism first received so much publicity, is examined first. I have looked at the way in which what happened at the end of the 1960s was linked to a long tradition, and how failure to conceive of feminism in political terms has led to a certain loss of energy, an impasse that some might deem to be failure. The GDR is examined next, since it offers a view of the role of women quite opposite to that which comes out of the American context. Moreover, western debates on the relationship between Marxism and feminism can be viewed from another perspective in the light of the new literary production by East German women writers. Then comes Italy, where the work of re-examining the whole question of the existence of a specifically women's culture is fairly advanced. Finally, I have looked at Britain, the country out of the four where women are still the most oppressed and where feminism has as many faces as the class system itself. But in Britain, whilst I was writing this book, a new phenomenon has arisen, one which offers an image of a radical alternative society. The women who have set up the peace camps have not only broken the barriers set up by the class system, they have also broken other artificially created barriers. Young and old, from all strata of society, defying conventional expectations of every kind, the women of the peace camps seem to suggest the viability of another way of life, conceived from another way of looking at the world. It is a return to a concept of society in which men and women, far from competing with each other, respect the differences they embody as distinct groups, even to the extent of speaking different languages.

My good fortune in enjoying the circumstances of a cosmopolitan childhood has enabled me to work in several languages. In Italy, I switch into Italian automatically, in the

GDR I work in German. Such languages can be learned by anyone with the time and the inclination. But the language of men, I have come to see, is a language that I cannot ever learn because its rules are closed to me by virtue of my experiences as a woman. It was perhaps predictable that I should have become fascinated by the work of those women who are trying to look at the universals of female cultures and languages, trying to discover whether the way in which a woman perceives the world differs from that of a man solely on account of social conditioning, on account of physiology, or on account of profound inner differences. And the attraction of this kind of work is that it is rooted in collectivity, not in subjective individuality. The existence of a women's culture can only be determined by women and by their collective voices speaking their separate language.

In making this statement I find myself face to face with the second problem basic to this book: that of finding a coherent place in the vast, ever-changing web of feminist activity. The similarities between women's movements in different societies are matched by the contrasts, and within each single social context there is now also a very wide age range, with women of my generation (the 1940s babies) being old enough to feel disillusioned by the failure of our hopes of twenty years ago, not old enough to take comfort from the evidence of cyclical changes as the generation preceding us can do, and yet too old to have acquired the toughness of the younger generations of women who have never known the naive delights of idealism. Older women who saw the failure of their dreams of a new world after the Second World War, and younger women who have to deal with a cruelly materialistic world in which unemployment and nuclear weapons are facts of daily life, are perhaps better equipped than my generation to keep up the struggle. In writing this book I have found it difficult not to give in to negative voices – to the voices that suggest that feminism and socialism no longer have a role to play in Western societies. And when I use the phrase 'giving in', what I mean by that is not so much that it is tempting actually to *believe* such a thing, but rather that it is hard to be pushed back out to the margins, back to what the establishment perceives as the lunatic fringe, when so many years of one's life have been spent watching those same marginal groups gradually moving towards the centre stage and believing that this time, for once, we might have been able to create a more egalitarian, more caring, more creatively humanitarian society across national boundaries.

My first experiences of the women's movement were in Italy in the student-revolutionary days of the late 1960s. I had gone back to Rome as a young lecturer in a left-wing department and quickly became involved in the student movement. In those days, our language was the language of radical political thought, but as groups of women began to meet and talk together so we ran up against the limitations of that language. I remember particularly the anti-Vietnam rallies in 1968, when women were singled out for beatings and manhandling, and how we came together afterwards to try to articulate our sense of rage and distress at the humiliation we had suffered not so much as comrades and as pacifists but as women. One detail that stays with me is the beating given to a woman colleague, who wet herself as she lay in the gutter unable to defend herself. Another is the storming of the Rome Arts Faculty by riot police, when we all escaped through rear windows of the building, and on our return some days later discovered that the ladies' lavatory had been hacked to bits with axes, both doors and porcelain bowls left in fragments. Such incidents marked a process of differentiation on the ground of sex that could not be ignored.

Italy in the late 1960s was full of confusions. Though I and my friends were all on the pill, we lived in a society that prized virginity so highly that women would pay large sums of money to have hymens rebuilt in private clinics. Some friends of mine, active in student politics, lived split existences; forbidden by the family to be out after eight o'clock at night, they were radicals by day, dutiful daughters in the evening. The youth movement of the Beatles era hit Italy particularly strongly, and almost overnight teenage consumerism boomed. Italy in the 1960s saw an unprecedented development of consumerism generally, as the rapid process of urbanization and industrialization changed the face of the nation. In the years that I lived in Rome, from the mid-1950s to the 1970s, the city grew from a centre with under a million inhabitants to a vast complex of jerry-built suburbs, with over three million people living within the perimeters of the expanding city, and vast shanty towns sprawling beneath costly new apartment blocks thrown up in what had previously been open countryside.

In this changing context, the old values clashed head-on with the new imported values – images of American life, and the pop-music world of Carnaby Street and Los Angeles, and, different but also profoundly powerful, the socialist Utopian images of Cuba and the China of the Cultural Revolution. That a strong women's movement should emerge from such a social context is not surprising, and that it should have been linked closely to the organized Left was also predictable. By the time we had learned the terminology of feminism from American women in the late 1960s, we had seen with a sense of surprise that we had been engaged in forming ourselves into a similar movement at the very same time, but with another political base.

However, when I first began to go to the United States, I was struck by the differences between American and Italian feminists rather than by their shared experiences. Of course there were parallels to be drawn between the civil rights campaign and the anti-war movement and the student–worker movements in Europe, all of which were happening around the same time, but the gaps between the two

8

societies were vast. I went to the United States following the European's myth of Otherness, looking for the society that is in constant movement. I had read my Sartre on American cities, and been intrigued by his analysis of the structure of those cities, with vast roads always leading one out and away from any possibility of lingering in a supposed centre. Los Angeles was just such a city, a place without a core, a huge sprawl of smaller, distinct cities joined in an amorphous whole. I married an American and tried to settle down.

The American marriage was brief and disastrous, although it lingered on for several years, during which we commuted across the Atlantic. The hopes of an alternative way of living evaporated almost instantly, and I came to feel myself a total stranger in a way that I had never felt in any European country. As soon as the opportunity arose, I went back to Europe, to England, and began another kind of life, this time with a child and a full-time job. During the years in the United States I had thrown myself into feminism in search of a lifeline – women's rap sessions, the La Leche League, therapy, neighbourhood women's groups. Reflecting on that period now, I can see that what I was undergoing was a period of post-natal depression, adjustment to the state of being married, learning to be a mother, coping with unexpected unemployment, and that these factors were the root of my unhappiness as much as the society in which I found myself trying to learn to live. I went to women's groups looking for some kind of shared experience, some kind of common factors that would help explain and alleviate the sense of loneliness and the feeling of not-belonging, of having no recognizable identity other than that of being someone's wife and someone's mother. Perhaps the fact that I had been so active politically and professionally before going to the States only made matters worse. Within the groups I found a sense of relief, but that kind of temporary help faded as soon as I found myself on my own again. Talking about the lack of orgasms never seemed to help me actually to relax enough to have one, just as all the practical advice and consolation from the La Leche League never did help me to get my dried-up breast milk flowing again after it had suddenly and traumatically stopped.

The unhappiness of my years in the States inevitably coloured my perceptions of American society. Living within it, yet feeling totally outside it, turning to other women and relating to them on one level whilst feeling deeply alienated from them on another, led me towards an analytical mode of discourse that perhaps comes through in my work today. I had gone from a society that saw individual action as necessarily part of a larger whole. The Mediterranean family, the Marxist politics of my upbring-ing, had fixed me with a concept of society in which the needs of the one exist in a dialectical relationship with the needs of the many. In the United States I found myself facing a truly alternative way of looking at the world. On the one hand, I was surprised by and grateful for the neighbourhood back-up services for women with families – the baby sitting circles, the coffee klatches, the school run, the help with supermarket shopping and so forth – but on the other hand, I was disturbed by the tendency in the women's groups towards what seemed to me to be a somewhat egotistic emphasis on self-development. Obsessed as I was with my own problems, I still could not orient myself in groups that were declaredly apolitical, stressing the needs for self-help and self-awareness. The pragmatic nature of American life was an alien form of existence. We talked at length about ourselves, our lives, our hopes and fears, we read Erica Jong and took out subscriptions to *MS*. But all the time I found questions growing in my mind – what next? Where to, after the ratification of the Equal Rights Amendment? What was the basis of pragmatic feminism? What were its limits?

My own limits were not very extensive. I came back to

Europe with a sense of homecoming, although even now I have nostalgia for the sheer beauty of North America, not of the cities about which I had imagined so much for so long, but of the great spaces of country with the vast differences in environment. In England I not only found a job, but I found the identity of being a single parent, working to support my small daughter and coming face to face with the negative attitudes of British society towards children. In England I became involved in a local crèche campaign, extended this to involvement in nursery action generally, and, perhaps because of the structure of British society, found that there were practical things I could do. I could collect signatures for petitions, stand in public places with a microphone talking to people, address public meetings, write letters. Almost without realizing it I became involved in the British women's movement at its grass-roots level, focusing on a particular need and working flat out in that one area. And again I went back to talking politics, linked myself with left-wing women's groups and felt more comfortable, more able to contribute something.

Shortly after my return to England, I made the first of many visits to the GDR. Gradually I developed friendships, took my daughter with me and my second daughter shortly after she was born, taught and gave lectures and slowly came to feel at home. Curiously perhaps, in spite of the differences in culture, I felt more at ease in East German society than I ever did in the United States.

The women's movement as such plays no part in life in the GDR, but I found many women to talk to whose experiences of trying to balance a profession and family life closely paralleled my own. These women, part of a new socialist society, nevertheless experienced the same sense of dislocation that I felt, and when I gave a public lecture in Berlin on 'Women in British Higher Education', the crowd, mainly of women, was so large that we had to transfer to a larger hall. At the end of the talk the dialogue between

myself and women in the audience was marvellous —
everyone was talking about the fundamental problem of the
relationship of a concept of feminism to Marxism in a way
that I had never encountered in western Europe. It was at
that talk that I met the woman who was to give me so much
help in researching the GDR section of this book by
organizing a visit for me some two years later to enable me
to meet women from all kinds of backgrounds and walks of
life. It was she who suggested that I might like to think of
writing up my experiences as a woman in different societies,
including a chapter on the GDR that she could help me
prepare.

The idea for the book began to germinate slowly. At first I
was aware of the absences in my experience — what I had
tended to see in all the societies in which I had lived were
those aspects of life that reflected who I was and where I
was coming from. As a result, the political basis of this book
is Marxist theory, the sexual bias is heterosexual, my deep
involvements have been with child-care campaigns and
mothers' rights campaigns and my interests are in the
creative arts generally, particularly in theatre. In short, I
have looked with the eyes of a heterosexual mother with
a left-wing middle-class intellectual education, simply because those were the eyes with which I had to see. Recog-
nizing my own limitations is one of the greatest lessons I feel
I have learned from women, and compensates now for any
sense I have of my inadequacy in the world at large.

My sense of the differences in the women's movement
across these four societies is therefore intensely personal
and reflects my own position. Had I not had children, had
I had physical relationships with women rather than deep
friendships, had I not been an intellectual on the Left, then
my whole sense of the societies would have been different.
My prejudices can be read between the lines, as can my
enthusiasms. Given an ideal choice, I would not live perma-
nently in the society in which I live now, but towards all

12

four societies I feel the attraction, the affection and the loathing of someone who cannot fully feel part of any of them, and yet is part of all. And in my sense of alienation, my sense of not belonging completely, I feel I am only experiencing a more extreme form of what so many women feel even when they *are* supposedly fully integrated members of a national culture, for cultural displacement is not only national, racial and religious in origin, it is also, I believe, sexual. The common ground that women in these four societies share is the no-woman's land of their female existence.

Notes

1 H. Hartmann, *The Unhappy Marriage of Marxism and Feminism: A Debate on Class and Patriarchy* (London: Pluto, 1981).

Chapter One

The United States

In August 1978 the American edition of *Cosmopolitan* featured an article by Betty Friedan, the 'Mother of the Movement', entitled provokingly 'Where are women in 1978?' In this unusually gloomy piece, a prelude to her controversial reconsideration of the women's movement *The Second Stage*[1], Friedan contrasts the nonchalant attitude of her daughter, who has just got into Harvard Medical School and who considers that feminism is already *passé*, with her own very personal doubts about exactly what the past decade of women's struggle has achieved. Friedan expresses her worries in her usual direct prose style:

'Hey, wait a minute', I want to say, 'it's not that simple, not yet . . .' For all this year and last, the signs have been adding up. Something is happening out there; the things we have fought so far to win are, one by one, being whittled away. The Supreme Court says companies don't have to pay women disability benefits for pregnancy and maternity leave. The California court says law schools and universities don't have to take 'affirmative action' to undo the discrimination that for generations has kept blacks and women out. The New York *Times* reports that the main cause of unemployment is the enormous increase of women entering the labor force, and that the wage gap between women and men is greater than before the women's movement began. Congress says the states don't have to let poor women use Medicaid funds to pay for abortions, no matter if the Supreme Court did say abortion was every woman's right. And in Nevada and Florida, North Carolina, Missouri, and Illinois, the state legislatures fail to ratify the Equal Rights Amendment, with less than a year left before time runs out next March to get the last three states of the thirty-eight needed to make it law. The hoopla of Houston, site of the National Women's Conference last November, kept women busy all year, hiding the real decline.

When Betty Friedan's first book, *The Feminine Mystique*, came out in 1963, a whole generation finally learned about the 'problem without a name', the sense of discontent and unease felt by American women whom the rest of the world considered to be in a position of unrivalled privilege. In the 1950s the antics of scatty sitcom women like Lucille Ball and the Hollywood mystique of the great, all-desirable female star had been joined to the image of the housewife whose chores were rendered almost non-existent by a plethora of labour-saving devices. The myth sold the idea that American women were both family-centred and yet freed from any sense of oppression. Over American woman-hood presided the great ideal, the President's wife, First Lady of the greatest land on earth. No presidential contender could afford to be seen without a graciously smiling wife beside him, his mainstay and helpmate, a model for all those American girls whose brothers believed in the possibility of one day becoming President in their own right. George Washington represented an ideal of honesty, integrity and male strength, while his wife, the aptly named Martha, represented the ideal of good wifehood.

Betty Friedan's book did much to shatter the Martha Washington idyll, and she dared to ask in public those questions that women had been asking in the privacy of their own homes. Was there to be nothing more in life than the ritualized abandonment of career in order to put a husband through college, the raising of children in hygienic surroundings, the steadily increased consumerism of middle-class expectations? What, ultimately, was it all for?

And how did it square with the rising divorce rate, with the high percentage of housewife alcoholics, with the sense of sterility of which so many women seemed to be tacitly aware in their lives?

After Betty Friedan's book – the deluge! Feminism escalated in the United States in the late 1960s and early 1970s in a way that left the rest of the world short of breath. The WITCH manifesto of 1968 was followed by the BITCH manifesto of a year later, while 1968 also saw Valerie Solanas, founder, theorist and sole member of SCUM (the Society for Cutting up Men), produce her manifesto, in which she proclaimed that 'Every man, deep down, knows he's a worthless piece of shit'.[2] And from the confusion of voices asserting a new aggressive role for those women who had been marginalized into passivity for too long, there emerged something the mass media could latch on to and mock: the image of the feminist woman as a bra-burner, publicly discarding the intimate items of female apparel as a gesture of contempt for femininity. It is curious to note how closely the image of the bra-burner, concocted by the media in the late 1960s, follows the pattern of the media-mockery of the nineteenth-century feminists who dared to follow Amalia Bloomer's example and wear baggy trousers instead of the impractical full skirts that the true lady was supposed to wear. In fact, the bra-burning tale seems to have originated with an early feminist protest, the New York Radical Women's Group attack on the Miss America pageant in 1968, when sisters were urged to throw into a huge Freedom Trash Can such things as bras, girdles, curlers, false eyelashes, wigs, magazines like *Cosmopolitan*, *Ladies Home Journal* and *Family Circle*, 'and any such woman-garbage you have around the house'.[3] But whatever its origins, the idea of the feminist as a bra-burner caught on and was exploited to the full. The polarization between the New Woman and Middle-American Ideal Woman was sharply exposed. The problem without a name was suddenly on everyone's lips. It had become headline material.

Yet ten years later, Betty Friedan was asking what had gone wrong. Was it possible that so much energy could have burned itself out so fast? Friedan was certainly clear in her mind that the demands of radical groups such as the early feminist Redstockings had certainly *not* been met. The Redstockings, in their 1969 manifesto, had concluded their statement with the following:

We call on all our sisters to unite with us in struggle. We call on all men to give up their male privileges and support women's liberation in the interest of our humanity and their own. In fighting for our liberation we will always take the side of women against their oppressors. We will not ask what is 'revolutionary' or 'reformist', only what is good for women.

The time for individual skirmishes has passed. This time we are going all the way.[4]

And the overreaction of the media, with the denigration of feminism and the spate of violent anti-women movies that followed close on the heels of the early manifestos, showed quite plainly that the new voice of American women was proving to be a very threatening one to the traditional status quo. With so much happening *for* women, then, with the example of American feminism spreading rapidly across western Europe, pioneering feminists like Betty Friedan must have thought that their wildest hopes were within the bounds of possibility. The bitterness with which Friedan upbraids her successful student daughter in her *Cosmopolitan* article is thus far more than a conflict between generations – it is the bitterness of a woman who is facing the betrayal of a life-time's work and beliefs:

I hope there will come a day when you, daughter mine, or your daughter, can truly afford to say 'I'm not a feminist. I'm a person' – and a day, not too far away, I hope, when I can stop fighting for women and get onto other matters that interest me now. I don't

17

like these new novels of Women's Liberation where, somehow, the heroines, after all their changing and developing, end up raped, murdered, suicides, or walking the beach alone – and none of the men are any good. When I tell Marilyn French, the author of that otherwise fine novel, *The Women's Room*, how strongly I object to such endings of our story, she says, 'How many women of our age can really move and not end up like that?' And so I think of the many women who have moved, whether from bitter necessity or new choice, and have ended up alone (but still would not go back) or have paid what seems to me too bitter a price. And I think how much better the endings are that may be possible for you, my daughter. But right now, you still have to pay your dues.

The discontented housewife for whom Betty Friedan's book provided a voice was not, of course, the prime mover of the revolution that turned into the women's movement. As the civil rights movement began to break up in the 1960s, the role of women activists became an increased focus for discussion. The tone of many of the early liberation manifestos reflects the sense of disenchantment many women felt with their male colleagues on the Left and in the civil rights movement; and there was a temptation to draw parallels with the Russian October Revolution, when the woman question began to emerge as a conflict in its own right once the basis for reconsidering all forms of social oppression was established.

After all, had not Lenin told Clara Zetkin that there were other, more difficult jobs to do before tackling the woman question? Moreover, he had made it perfectly clear that while he was concerned to break the power of property relations over women, discussions on sexuality were irrelevant. 'I ask you is this the time to keep working women busy for months at a stretch with such questions as how to love or be loved, how to woo or be wooed?', he wrote to her in 1920.[5] The disenchantment that women had felt in revolutionary Russia provided an apt parallel with the frustrations of American women nearly fifty years later.

The emergence of a separate women's struggle in the 1960s coincided with the emergence of new assertiveness by a range of oppressed groups – blacks, chicanos, American Indians, what Marlene Dixon had called the 'whole soft underbelly' of American society.[6] The prospect of minority groups locked in conflict with a dominant colonial power offered a model for feminism which, for a time at least, identified with other groups. But as realization dawned that women were not a minority group by any stretch of the imagination and, moreover, that black women and chicano women were equally oppressed by their male comrades, the tenuous front of solidarity began to fragment. In their useful book *Rebirth of Feminism*, Judith Hole and Ellen Levine report a statement by a politico woman working in a collective:

Feminism is subject to racial and class issues and therefore the idea that we're all sisters, we all have the same problems, is bullshit. Don't tell me that there's no difference between a woman who can hardly feed her kids and that of a comfortable surburban housewife with her maid.[7]

The key to understanding the progress of the women's movement in the United States lies in accepting the fact of fragmentation from the very start. There is no single unified movement and there has never been one. The early years of feminism reveal a range of voices, from the intellectual moderates, such as Gloria Steinem and Betty Friedan, to the extremes of small far-left or fringe groups, with all kinds of other voices speaking in between. One of the most entertaining of these voices was that of the various WITCH covens, which began to emerge in 1968 and spread across the country. 'There is no "joining" WITCH,' declared the New York manifesto. 'If you are a woman and dare to look within yourself, you are a Witch. You make your own rules'.[8] Groups of WITCH members appeared from time to time to perform public hexings of organizations and individuals guilty of oppression of women, and the staginess of some of these events stands out even at a time of frequent public demonstration. The New York founding coven incorporated theatricality in its frame of reference, declaring that:

> WITCH is in all women, everything.
> It's theater, revolution,
> Magic, terror and joy.
> It's an awareness that witches and gypsies
> Were the first guerrilla and resistance fighters
> Against oppression – the oppression of women,
> Down through the ages.[9]

The common concern of all the voices is plainly the fact of the oppression of women, but the differences are revealed when we consider the styles of action and the theoretical bases. The oppression of women could not be comfortably linked with the phenomenon of minority-group oppression, just as it could not be comfortably tied to patterns of class oppression – and the class problem in the United States is a peculiarly American minefield of complexities in its own right.

Whereas the British class system is rigidly predetermined and provides categories into which individuals are slotted, the American class system is more flexible and therefore less easy to define. Since class is understood differently, it is possible to move through the American class system and to cross boundaries in ways that would be impossible in the British context. What further confuses matters is the use of the term *class* by British and American feminists as though they were discussing the same thing, whilst in fact the term only becomes meaningful in context and is effectively untranslatable between the two cultures. Intellectual feminists could properly be said to have emerged from a middle-class tradition, and that tradition was most likely to be white, but as black Americans joined the ranks of the middle classes in legions, the question of black women's emancipation increased in complexity also. Black women activists pointed out that discrimination against them in the area of labour relations, for example, was far more strongly marked than that practised against white women. Black women, and, once they began to make their case known also, chicano women, formed the category of lowest wage-earners in the United States, even though the tradition of black women working was of long standing. In 1930, for example, at a time when black women were largely employed as agricultural workers and domestic servants, two in five black women worked in contrast to only one in five white women. Black activists began to look at the history of their oppression and define themselves as 'slaves of slaves' in a pyramid model, in which the white male was Oppressor Number One, embodying as he did the capitalist system that maintained his power, with white women, black men and finally black women below him in descending order.

In her book *The Dialectic of Sex*, subtitled *The Case for Feminist Revolution*, Shulamith Firestone has an important chapter on 'Racism: the Sexism of the Family of Man'. She discusses the tensions and contradictions involving the black woman – solidarity with the black man against white racism, but conflict with him over sexist roles she is expected to fulfil; solidarity with the white woman against the phenomenon of male oppression, but conflict with her over issues of race. Firestone devises an image of conflict to illustrate these contradictions. Racism, she argues, is sexism extended; it is a form of the eternal triangle, in which the white man is husband, the white woman is wife and the black woman is the Other Woman. This situation inevitably leads to tension between the women who are asked to play vastly different roles with the Husband, and it leads to the Husband living out a dichotomy between respectability and the moral values of the traditional family on the one hand

21

and passion and the forbidden on the other. Firestone then asks:

If, in the white man's sex drama, the white woman plays Wife (his private property), and the black woman plays Whore (his public property), what role does the black man play? The black man plays Pimp. The black man is a pawn in the game of the white man's sexuality.[10]

In this role, the black man becomes the agent of the black woman's exploitation, and her coexistence with him is founded on a basic contradiction. Whatever the unity that may be achieved between black man and black woman, it is undermined by their relationship with white man. For, by casting the black man in the role of Pimp, the white man both uses him and fears him; hence the long tradition of black men as sexual outsiders, waiting in the darkness to attack white man through his most treasured possession, his white woman.

Shulamith Firestone's analogy is interesting because it illustrates the importance of dialectical thinking and shows something of the complexities of the issues. Her approach is in marked contrast to the idealistic 'all women are sisters' voices that were heard in the 1960s, but by 1970 idealism was fading out of American public life. The alternative society of love, beauty and freedom that many had genuinely believed in had long since foundered on the rocks of commercial exploitation. The flower children of the mid-1960s became the ageing hippies of the 1970s, unwilling to look closely at a society in the process of moving to the Right. The many voices of feminism, like the multiplying voices of radicalism, became less coherent as the scale of the problems grew. Around the same time the voices of anti-feminism began to be raised, preaching a return to the traditional areas of women's power – the family circle and the bedroom, where women rule as guardians of the moral and emotional life of the nation.

Against the emergence of the new Right which came to form a fairly united oppositional front, the fragmentation of the women's movement showed up all the more clearly. And with fragmentation came a growing sense of disenchantment. By January 1981, Gloria Steinem noted in *MS* that opinion polls after the election of Ronald Reagan showed the biggest sex gap in any presidential election since 1952, with men constituting 54 per cent, and women 37 per cent of those favouring the newly inaugurated President. Only about 49 per cent of the voters were women, and, since women of voting age outnumber men (53 per cent of the voters in the 1976 election that put Jimmy Carter into the White House were women), the 1980 figures mark a very sharp change indeed. If women were too bored or too tired to register even a protest vote, what had happened to the energy of the early years of feminism? Had the rot set in so far that there could not even be concerted action against the most reactionary US President of the post-1945 era? Gloria Steinem also warned that the Moral Majority was celebrating Reagan's victory.

So are right-to-lifers, supporters of the death penalty, nuclear energy enthusiasts and Stop ERA leaders. And they should be. They were organized, and the majority forces, including feminists, were not.

A few months earlier, writing in the *Observer* of 19 October 1980, Katherine Whitehorne had reported on the organization of women's groups in the United States and came to the same conclusions. The feminist groups, based on collective organizational principles, appeared less coherent than the mass of right-wing groups emerging on all sides:

Outfits called Women Who Want to be Women, the Stop ERA movement and the pro-lifers – in this language, pro-life means anti-abortion and pro-choice its opposite. You also get some strange cross-breeds like Mormons for ERA (official Mormon policy is against), Catholics for Choice (ditto) or Feminists for

Life; I haven't yet come across Communists for Reagan, the Ku Klux Blacks or Foetuses for Choice, but such is the rich variety of this country that even that wouldn't surprise me.

She rather facetiously pinpoints the problem that a European woman has when considering American feminism; for just as the image of the American woman was marketed throughout the world in the 1950s as an ideal for all to follow, so the American feminist was marketed through the 1970s. When British women were still struggling to gain equal pay for equal work, Americans were pushing for positive discrimination. When European feminists were founding tiny magazines that they wrote, printed and distributed themselves, American feminist magazines printed on glossy paper with stunning lists of contents and expensive subscription charges kept filtering across the Atlantic. When, in 1967, together with a handful of feminist colleagues, I wore trousers to teach my classes at the University of Rome in contravention of regulations, this seemed a major advance for women's rights. During the winter of 1970 at a Midwestern campus I didn't see a woman in a skirt until the spring came. American feminists seemed to be light years ahead. And yet they failed to oppose Reagan and silence the new right. Somewhere something was not working out. Could American feminism also be a media invention, one began to wonder, especially when the Women's Novel became a million-dollar industry and *MS* ran cigarette advertisements suggesting the 'You've come a long way, baby'? Moreover, in spite of the proliferation of women's studies courses in higher education and of books by, for and about women, nothing seemed to be coming from the United States in the way of intellectual feminism. The theoretical debates were established in Europe and have remained in Europe, and there is no American equivalent of Julia Kristeva or Luce Irigaray or Maria Antoinetta Macciocchi or Sheila Rowbotham. At the same time, because of the fragmentation of the American feminist voice, it is difficult for anyone outside to have much idea of what is actually going on. Katherine Whitehorne pokes fun at what seems to European eyes to be an American penchant for extremist views, but she is also acutely aware of the difficulty of talking about an American women's movement without falling into gross generalizations and erroneous assumptions.

Yet in spite of the many voices of American feminism, it is possible to determine consistent lines, to isolate areas of continued interest and development. Charlotte Bunch, radical lesbian feminist, argued in an important article entitled 'Beyond either/or: feminist options',[11] that the women's movement was fragmenting into three dominant and often mutually exclusive trends: socialist feminism, political reformism and cultural or spiritual separatism. Now, several years later, it is possible to look behind Charlotte Bunch's tripartite division and to see that the dominant lines of feminist development are twofold: the one being the search, from a variety of starting points, for alternative organizational structures, and the other being a reassessment of the cultural and spiritual role of women – a sort of feminist metaphysics.

Mary Daly's *Gyn/Ecology* concludes with an extraordinary image of the new women's consciousness in action:

As we feel the empowerment of our own Naming we hear more deeply our call of the wild. Raising pairs of arms into the air we expand them into shells, sails. Splashing our legs in the water we move our oars. Our beautiful, spiral-like designs are the designs/ purposes of our bodies/minds. We communicate these through our force-fields, our auras, our O-Zones. We move backward over the water, toward the Background. We gain speed. Argonauts move apart and together, forming and re-forming our Amazon Argosy. In the rising and setting of our sister sun, we seek the gold of our hearts' desire. In the light of our sisters the moon and stars we rekindle the Fore-Crones' fire. In its searing light we see through the father's lies of genesis and demise; we burn through the snarls of the Nothing-Lovers. In the beginning was not the word. In the beginning is the hearing. Spinsters spin deeper into the listening deep. We can spin only what we hear, because we hear, and as well as we hear. We can weave and unweave, knot and unknot, only because we hear, what we hear, and as well as we hear. Spinning is celebration/cerebration. Spinsters Spin all ways, always. Gyn/Ecology is Un-Creation; Gyn/Ecology is Creation.[12]

The cult of matriarchy, the emphasis on the primeval healing powers of women, and the campaigns for the ordination of women within established ecclesiastical organizations derive ultimately from the same source. At first glance there may not seem to be much in common between a radical Roman Catholic nun opposed to the Church's stand on birth control and celibacy of the clergy and a woman like Jeannine Parvati, author of *Hygieia: A Woman's Herbal*[13] who provides, among other fascinating pieces of advice, recipes for the ritual cooking of human placenta. What links them is their common awareness of the spiritual dimension of American society, a phenomenon that has been much discussed and much questioned, and which is in marked contrast to the rationalist tendency of European intellectual life. The language of religiosity recurs in the most (to European minds) unexpected places. In Catherine Stimpson's review of Betty Friedan's *The Second Stage*,[14] for example, the central metaphor is biblical. Friedan's second book is described as her New Testament, with her first book as the Old Testament, and we are told that the author has 'revised her vision of history to offer us her gospel and our redemption'. Such terminology recalls the extravagant use of biblical references and imagery by nineteenth-century feminist speakers as part of their rhetorical apparatus. It is, of course, not insignificant that the crusading rhetoric of abolitionism should so closely parallel that of the civil rights and anti-Vietnam War campaigns over a century later.

In the early years of feminism, anti-rationalism did

actually square with one of the attempts at alternative organizational structures – the establishment of the consciousness-raising group. In the Redstockings manifesto of 1969 the emphasis is on the intimate relationship between personal experience and political action (the personal is political):

Our chief task at present is to develop female class consciousness through sharing experience and publicly exposing the sexist foundation of all our institutions. Consciousness-raising is not 'therapy', which implies the existence of individual solutions and falsely assumes that the male–female relationship is purely personal, but the only method by which we can ensure that our program for liberation is based on the concrete realities of our lives. The first requirement for raising class consciousness is honesty, in private and in public, with ourselves and other women.[15]

Early consciousness-raising sessions may be compared to religious meetings, in which the absence of predetermined leadership forced women into introducing themselves through confessional statement. Moreover, the existence of these groups implied a common link among women that marked out certain areas as their own, apart from male experience. And in that separateness, the subject that came to the fore was the vast one of sexuality.

In her introduction to her anthology of writings from the women's movement *Sisterhood is Powerful*, Robin Morgan asked the question that was to preoccupy the next decade of American feminists: what are the alternatives to the family structures of contemporary society? She went on to be more specific:

Living alone? Living in mixed communes with men and women? Living in all-women communes? Having children? Not having children? Raising them collectively, or in the old family structure? The father and/or other men sharing equally in child care, or shouldering it entirely, or not being permitted any participation? Homosexuality as a viable political alternative which straight women must begin to recognize as such? More – homosexuality, or bisexuality, as a beautiful affirmation of human *sexuality*, without all those absurd prefixes? Test-tube births? Masturbation? Womb transplants? Gender control of the foetus? . . . Parthenogenesis? Why? Why not?[16]

She enumerates some of the issues that dominated consciousness-raising groups in the early years of the movement, the issues that transcended the nitty-gritty discussion of what kind of overt political action to take. With non-centralized groups taking a strongly anti-authoritarian, anti-programmatic stance, women increasingly turned away from activity in the social and political sphere and turned their attention towards the definition of alternative personal structures, in which sexuality acquired a quasi-mystical dimension. This emphasis is one of the most strikingly individualistic features of American feminism, for although the issues of a woman's right to define and control her own sexuality have featured prominently in women's movements elsewhere, the focus has been different. The long-running campaigns to legalize abortion, for example, that have dominated European feminism throughout the 1970s do not have similar mass counterparts in the United States. Of course, the American abortion campaign has been of considerable importance, but it has been subsumed under a wider perspective of sexual reorientation. From the United States has come the great debate over the vaginal orgasm; Shere Hite's *Report on Female Sexuality* and her follow-up book on male sexuality; the re-examination of the mother–daughter relationship that runs through new feminist writing, theatre, art and film as a dominant motif; and, of course, the lesbian separatist debate over whether heterosexuality as the norm reinforces male supremacy. Moreover, the wide-ranging discussions on rape and sexual harassment that preoccupy American feminists have also tended to concentrate on male versus female sexuality, rather than to examine male violence against women as European feminists seem to have preferred to do as a basis for their analysis of other issues.

It is obvious that questions of sexuality must be central to any feminist movement. I am not trying to imply that such questions should in any way be put into second place, but the particular American emphasis on sexuality is indeed striking. In the early 1970s, American feminists with whom I had contact were intensely preoccupied with talking about sexuality. When we met, discussion always moved towards the difficulties we might have encountered in our sex lives; and for the first time many of us began to look again at our sexual feelings towards other women. Questions of sexual fulfilment seemed extraordinarily important, and sexual freedom for woman was easily mistaken for liberation. Exchanging partners as frequently as men had been allowed to do, demanding complete gratification whenever, wherever and with whomsoever one chose, being totally in control of the sexual situation, was the image of emancipation initially offered by magazines such as *Cosmopolitan* and *Playgirl* and much discussed in the women's groups. And the extent to which such discussions did dominate was clear to me when I compared my experiences in the United States with those in Italian and British groups, in which the emphasis was on a socialist concept of feminism and the discussion revolved around localized support for national feminist campaigns together with the search for an intellectual base of feminism.

But if American feminists in the early years were deeply concerned with questions of sexuality, some were also intent on organizing grass-roots political issues on a national scale. NOW (National Organization of Women) was set up by Betty Friedan and colleagues in 1966 and grew to become the largest American women's organization. Its goal was:

to take action to bring women into full participation in the mainstream of American society *now*, exercising all the privileges and responsibilities thereof in truly equal partnership with men.[17]

Achieving that truly equal partnership involved a rethinking of traditional marriage, with its assumptions about the secondary nature of work for women outside the home, and a restructuring of the man's role within the family as part of a move towards the sharing of responsibility for the home and participation in child care. NOW also protested against the misrepresentation of women in the media and the discrimination enshrined in all the major social institutions. In short, the rhetoric of NOW's earliest statements advocated a belief in the universality of the need for women's emancipation and a commitment to fighting for equality within the law. It was the manifesto of liberal feminism.

Within months dissension began to emerge within NOW, inevitably perhaps, because of the vastness and vagueness of the range of issues it sought to encompass. The two most controversial issues of the second conference in Washington in 1967 were abortion and the Equal Rights Constitutional Amendment (ERA), and although a Bill of Rights[18] for woman was drawn up that covered both these, serious divisions over politics and tactics had begun to appear.

The abortion issue led to the first major public split in 1968, when Ti-Grace Atkinson, president of the New York chapter of NOW, left to form the October 17th Movement, later renamed the Feminists. She protested against the lack of commitment of NOW to abortion, but more seriously she questioned its hierarchical organizational structures, declaring that:

I realize that by holding these offices I am participating in oppression itself. You cannot destroy oppression by filling the position of the oppressor. I don't think you can fight oppression from the inside. Since I have failed to get rid of these power positions I hold, I have no choice but to step out of them.[19]

Two years later, in 1970, NOW was accused of having a heterosexual bias, and although it eventually came to support lesbian rights, the debates illuminated the pre-dominantly heterosexual bias of the leadership. Moreover, other gaps could be seen – the division between women of Friedan's generation and younger NOW members, and the essentially white middle-class bias of the founder members compared with the membership at large.

The essential, white, heterosexual middle classness of NOW, which continued, although in diluted form, through-out the 1970s, was matched by other groups such as the Women's Equality Action League. The Professional Women's Caucus, set up in 1970, was established on more radical principles, but still reflected the predominantly middle-class intellectual bias of its origins. But the point over which a whole range of groups were able to come together in unanimity was the issue that has dominated organized American feminism for a decade: the attempt to pass the Equal Rights Constitutional Amendment.

The ERA was first introduced to Congress in 1923. It reads:

Section I: Equality of Rights under the law shall not be denied or abridged by the United States or by any state on account of sex.

Section II: The Congress shall have the power to enforce by appropriate legislation, the provisions of this article.

Section III: This amendment shall take effect two years after the date of ratification.

The history of the ERA is one of continued failure. It died in committee in 1923, 1928, 1931, 1932 and 1933. It emerged again in 1938, and in 1945 it got as far as the House of Representatives. In 1946 the Senate failed to get the necessary two-thirds majority to send the ERA to the states for consideration and, though it was finally approved in 1950, a floor amendment by Senator Carl Hayden (the 'Hayden rider') kept all state protective legislation intact and so effectively nullified the amendment's effect. Finally, after a further series of vicissitudes, the ERA cleared the

Senate in March 1972 and was sent to the states for ratification. Almost immediately, organized opposition to the ratification of the amendment began, with Phyllis Schlafly's ubiquitous STOP ERA movement and HOT DOGS (Humanitarians Opposed to the Degradation of Our Daughters), a Utah-based women's organization.

Organized opposition by women's groups to the ERA gained ground, and Phyllis Schlafly's campaign was successful in persuading several states either to refuse to ratify or, in the case of Nebraska and Tennessee, to rescind ratification. The basis of the anti-ERA campaign seemed to be fear that a woman's right to choose to work would be replaced with a notion of mandatory work and that the institution of the family would be destroyed to the detriment of women. A woman was 'entitled to be protected and provided for in her career as a woman, wife and mother',[20] Schlafly argued in her 1972 report, and her interpretation of the role of women had the backing of many women in religious organizations. It also had the backing of Ronald Reagan and his First Lady, Nancy, who added their weight to the general anti-feminist feeling in circulation by the end of the 1970s. Yet, significantly, even that anti-feminism has undergone certain changes. Much has been made of the changing image of Nancy Reagan herself. Seen as the adoring, retiring President's wife, who fixed her husband with the now famous glassy-eyed gaze of admiration whenever he appeared in public, in the first years of his first term of office, she had become a very different persona by 1984. Whatever her role as political adviser in private, she had become a public figure, deeply involved in issues such as juvenile drug abuse; and, instead of the submissive wife image, what we had was the image of a capable, hard-working companion. Out went the reports of Nancy's extravagant spending on clothes and household china; instead the media focused on her work as presidential helpmate, an image summed up by her visit to Mexico in the wake of the disastrous earthquake of 1985 as an unofficial US ambassador acting in her husband's stead.

The anti-ERA campaign and the insistence of the new Right on the traditional values of woman as homemaker, companion and mother, who has a right to protection from the darker side of life, appears at first sight to be absurdly old-fashioned in a country that so prides itself on its modernity. But if we consider what the demand for 'protection' means in relation to, for example, the more liberal divorce laws that many states have instituted, it is possible to see that the appeal is to fears that are far from imaginary. The notion of no-fault divorce, seen at first as a step in the right direction, towards greater freedom of choice, has led to an increased amount of hardship for women, most predominant amongst whom is the middle-aged housewife who suddenly finds herself being divorced by the husband who has provided for her for years and who has frequently also prevented her from fulfilling her career potential. When children are involved, such cases become even more difficult. Liberal US divorce laws are not backed up by increased child-care and social-security provision, and in recent years a growing number of judges have awarded custody to fathers, especially in cases in which there is economic disparity between parents. So the un-employed mother whose work has been entirely within the home, the woman suffering from Friedan's 'problem without a name', who finds herself being divorced by her husband may also lose custody of her children by virtue of his greater financial reliability and social status. It is all very well to argue that raising the housewife's consciousness will alter the way she perceives her situation, but the plain facts are that an ironic side-effect of the feminist demand for a realignment of roles within the family has led to men having greater rights as fathers at women's expense. And the women most likely to suffer are those to whom the moral Right appeals, those who never go near a consciousness-raising session and who cannot conceive of lesbians being mothers. It is small wonder that they have come to see feminism as against their own interests. So long as they can cling to some vestige of the idea of protection, there is less risk, they feel, of being cast out into the wilderness by the supposed protector. We have only to think of the extra-ordinary success in the peak years of the women's move-ment, of films such as *Paper Moon*, with the counterpart relationship in real life between the father and daughter protagonists, Ryan and Tatum O'Neil, or *Kramer vs. Kramer*, to see how great the emotional impact of a centralized father–child relationship can be. The mother in such films is marginalized, and in the case of *Kramer vs. Kramer* the marginalization is particularly insidious, because the mother, in spite of the manipulative, negative presentation of her actions, does not callously abandon her child but goes off to try to find herself with new feminist awareness. At the roots, there is no ideological difference between the image of the ideal heterosexual family in the television commercials and the image of the caring neo-feminist father who takes over the mother's role while she searches for more personal space: in both scenarios the woman is secondary.

In 1982 the Oklahoma State Senate refused to ratify the ERA, and the cause was lost yet again. In the January 1983 issue of *MS*, a special report on the collapse of the ratification of the ERA significantly failed to explain what had gone wrong. Nationally, the report argued, the ERA failed because:

– too many people, both men and women, dislike women;
– most of the majority expressing support in the polls remained, at best, complacently expectant instead of becoming politi-cally insistent; and
– the opposition was better organized.

The questions that were not answered were the same that

might have been put in Britain after the Conservative Party returned to power for the second term in 1983; why do women support right-wing policies in such large numbers? Is it simply a question of complacency, and of the power of big-business interests backing up the establishment, or might there have been a serious miscalculation by feminists about the extent to which the notion of the role of women in society was changing?

The silliness of Phyllis Schlafly's rhetoric disguised the extent to which the new Right was organizing opposition to the ERA on more substantial intellectual grounds. The ERA campaign came to be linked to the abortion issue, and the whole question of women's rights became enmeshed with the problem of the role of the state in matters of welfare. The effect of these right-wing tactics was to confuse equal rights for women with issues that involved strong religious or moral views, thereby deterring large numbers of women from supporting the ERA on grounds that had nothing to do with the amendment itself. The John Birch Society had early on perceived the ERA campaign as a danger to the American Way of Life, and in 1980 the Republican Party finally withdrew support for the ERA, a move which heralded its final defeat.

Zillah Eisenstein, in her book *The Radical Future of Liberal Feminism*, argued that the ERA was a 'necessary but not sufficient strategy for feminists'. She presented the ERA as a first step in the process of understanding 'the built-in inequality of the economic class structure and patriarchal system we lived in', a position clearly perceived by the new Right as one to be opposed at all costs.[21] The problem of ratifying the ERA seems, therefore, to have connections with the depoliticized nature of much of American feminism. In other words, the far-reaching revolutionary consequences of ratifying the ERA seem not to have been widely understood by those in favour, and to have been widely over-emphasized by those against. The post-Second World War period produced the McCarthyite old Right; the post-Vietnam period produced the new Right, whose focus of antagonism was not so much the red menace as the menace within the home.

In the richest country in the world, the country where soup kitchens have come back into existence with rising unemployment and collapse of the decaying inner cities, the ratification of the ERA could have had repercussions both in regard to the labour market and in regard to the welfare services. The economic crisis at home, the tarnished reputation in world politics, the evidence of government corruption, combined to produce a context in which greater security was needed. Fear of the dissolution of the family and of sexuality began to rise to the surface in the new climate of disillusionment. The rejection of the ERA was therefore based not so much on dislike or fear of women as on fear of change, on the need to reassert the old values that had come to signify comfort and safety. Zillah Eisenstein was quite right in suggesting that the ERA was a first step in a revolutionary process, but American society as a whole was not ready to begin the process.

In her analysis of liberal feminism, Zillah Eisenstein suggests that the term is contradictory, since feminism is potentially subversive of the capitalist patriarchal state and hence of liberalism itself. She is careful not to dismiss the achievements of liberal feminism as a first stage, but she warns against taking an ahistorical attitude to feminism:

Let women learn from the American feminists of the nineteenth century, who were clearly liberal, yet radical for their time. Let feminists learn from these early mistakes.[22]

Contemporary feminism ignores its own history at its peril is Eisenstein's message, and the point she makes is very convincing indeed. In tracing the development of the mid-twentieth-century women's movement back to the civil rights movements of the early 1960s, people all too easily forget that nineteenth-century American feminism was both advanced and widespread. Betty Friedan's *The Feminine Mystique* puts substantially the same case that had been put by Charlotte Perkins Gilman in her *Women and Economics*, published in 1898, and Charlotte Perkins Gilman in her turn was able to draw on a large body of work that had been appearing steadily over the previous fifty years, ever since the first Women's Rights Convention at Seneca Falls, New York, in 1848.

The Seneca Falls convention was an extraordinary phenomenon. The history of its genesis has been well documented and, as has often been pointed out, the way to Seneca Falls was paved with abolition, temperance and revival meetings. In their great six-volume *History of Woman Suffrage*,[23] Elizabeth Cady Stanton, Susan B. Anthony and Matilda Joslyn Gage identify the World Anti-Slavery Convention of 1840, held in London, as the great turning-point in the development of American feminism. At this conference the American women delegates were refused seats on account of their sex, even though they were representatives of the American Anti-Slavery Society, and the angry reverberations of this occasion led to increased feminist militancy. The announcement of the Seneca Falls convention (issued without signature by Lucretia Mott, Martha C. Wright, Elizabeth Cady Stanton and Mary Ann McClintock) declared that the convention would discuss the social, civil and religious condition and rights of women. During the first day there was to be a closed meeting, 'exclusively for women'. After Seneca Falls, Women's Rights Conventions were held almost every year up to the beginning of the Civil War in different cities across the eastern and Midwestern states.

In her anthology of documents and introductory critical essays, *The Feminist Papers*, Alice Rossi discusses the nineteenth-century feminists in terms of two groups: Enlightenment feminists and moral-crusader feminists. In the first group she places Frances Wright, Margaret Fuller, Harriet Martineau and John Stuart Mill, and in the second group she places Lucretia Mott, Sarah and Angelika Grimke, Elizabeth Cady Stanton, Susan B. Anthony, Lucy Stone and Antoniette Brown. The difference between the two groups, according to Alice Rossi, is that the Enlightenment feminists were 'highly urban, sophisticated, solitary thinkers and writers', whereas the moral-crusader feminists were almost all native-born middle-class Americans from rural areas or small towns. She claims that the former group tended to be solitary workers, whilst the latter were 'joiners':

Elizabeth Stanton's impulse was to give a 'call', hold meetings, draw up resolutions, form local societies to implement those resolutions, and organize the network of local societies into a national organization.[24]

It is not too difficult to extend Alice Rossi's distinction between the two groups beyond the nineteenth century as the continuing basis for the two main lines of contemporary American feminism. Margaret Fuller's concept of feminism involved a metaphysical dimension. In her piece in *The Dial*, she proclaimed:

The special genius of woman I believe to be electrical in movement, intuitive in function, spiritual in tendency. She is great not so easily in classification, or re-creation, as in an instinctive seizure of causes, and a simple breathing out of what she receives that has the singleness of life, rather than the selecting or energizing of art.[25]

In contrast to Margaret Fuller's intellectual feminism were the great campaigns of the mid-nineteenth century, the abolitionist campaigns and later the temperance and suffrage movements. Sarah Grimke's impassioned rhetoric appeals not so much to the intellect as to the gut reactions of women faced with the evidence of the evils of slavery:

Nor does the coloured woman suffer alone: the moral purity of

The United States

the white woman is deeply contaminated. In the daily habit of seeing the virtue of her enslaved sister sacrificed without hesitancy or remorse, she looks upon the crimes of seduction and illicit intercourse without horror, and although not personally involved in the guilt, she loses that value for innocence in her own, as well as the other sex, which is one of the strongest safeguards to virtue.[26]

As in the 1960s, feminism and civil rights were intricately connected. The difference, of course, lies in the totally different contexts of those two campaigns, so that Elizabeth Cady Stanton could argue for women's suffrage by proclaiming the greater virtues of middle-class women over semi-literate immigrants and negros. 'Would you compel the women of New York to sue the Tweeds, the Sweeneys, the Connollys for their inalienable rights,' she asked, 'or to have the scales of justice balanced for them in the unsteady hand of a Cardozo, a Barnard, or a McGunn?'[27] Women may have been pro-abolition, but, coming as they did from middle-class backgrounds, they were quick to uphold classist and élitist social concepts. The voice of Sojourner Truth, a black former slave woman, was a uniquely individualistic one. At the Akron, Ohio, convention in 1851, Sojourner Truth's oratorical skills were beyond compare. 'From God and a woman! Man had nothin' to do wid Him!'[28] But Sojourner Truth did not have a white middle-class intellectual background.

Throughout the nineteenth century, American women seemed to be gaining enormous ground over their European counterparts. Oberlin College, the first to admit women and to grant them a regular arts degree, was founded in 1833 and opened its doors to women in 1841. Other, all-women establishments followed: Vassar opened in 1865, Smith and Wellesley in 1875 and Bryn Mawr in 1885. Full political equality for women was decreed in Wyoming in 1869, and in 1890 Wyoming entered the union as the first state with full suffrage for women. Colorado followed suit in 1893 and Utah and Idaho in 1896, though no other state enfranchised its women until Washington in 1910. It is interesting, of course, that the first states to grant women the vote were the newly settled states, and such books as Dee Brown's *Women of the Wild West*[29] document the great resilience of the early women settlers whose contribution has been outweighed by the myths of male conquest perpetuated by the Hollywood cinema.

In spite of lengthy widespread campaigns and in spite of a sizeable body of theoretical writings, feminism, in the United States gradually moved not only out of the public eye but also out of the consciousness of millions of women, so that by the 1920s the movement was all but played out. The question remains as to whether the growth of feminism in the 1960s was therefore a rebirth, a resurgence of a movement that already had a history, or whether it was something completely new. The parallels between nineteenth-century feminism and liberal feminism in the mid-twentieth century are strikingly close, with intellectual feminists such as Kate Millet, Adrienne Rich and Charlotte Bunch in the line of Enlightenment feminism, and with Betty Friedan, Gloria Steinem and NOW in the line of moral-crusader feminists. Moreover, both movements drew their strength essentially from a middle-class base and both threw up a mass of contradictions. The abolition, suffrage and temperance campaigns revealed the early feminists' WASP (White Anglo-Saxon Protestant) origins, and the leadership of twentieth-century American feminism reveals a similar bias. In an article entitled 'Race and class: beyond personal politics', Beverly Fisher-Manick notes that feminist analysis of the family has tended to focus on the middle-class nuclear family unit and questions some of its basic assumptions:

Consciousness raising is a valuable cornerstone of feminist theory and practice. But as a verbal exercise in self-examination and group sharing, it is also an approach with a class and race bias.

White middle-class women are comfortable with a form that relies mainly on verbal skills. Women of other races and classes are not as comfortable in situations that stress group process. I'm not saying that Third World women and working- and lower-class women can't express themselves verbally. I'm saying that the formality of using CR as a technique for communication is stifling and intimidating to women who are accustomed to expressing themselves in less defined and directed forms.[30]

It is perhaps not so surprising that the ERA should have become a vehicle for liberal feminism in much the same way as universal suffrage became a talking point for nineteenth-century feminism. By focusing on one cause it is possible to sweep complications and contradictions temporarily under the carpet, to read tokenism as a sign of successful infiltration of the social system. The difficulties begin when the mass cause is removed, and the decline of the nineteenth-century movement seems to have coincided, roughly speaking, with the granting of the vote to women across the country in 1920 and with the increased militancy of the American working class. In 1919, Anna Howard Shaw, a leader of the suffrage campaign told a younger woman, Emily Newell Blair: 'I'm sorry for you young women who have to carry on the work for the next ten years, for suffrage was a symbol, and now you have lost your symbol.'[31] When the labour movement, in which many women became active, began to organize in the major industrialized areas, it was clear that a middle-class feminist movement had little part to play. Emma Goldman, whose autobiography gives a powerful and moving account of the labour struggles in the first years of the twentieth century, pointed out that the suffrage campaign was founded on faulty, idealistic premises. 'There is no hope even that woman, with her right to vote, will ever purify politics', Goldman claimed,[32] suggesting that woman could not succeed where man had so patently failed. Although she saw women's suffrage as a useful step, she realized that revolution should be perceived as a process rather than simply as the reform of some individual laws within the existing social and economic system.

The women garment workers' strike of 1909–10 showed the increased organization of working-class women as more entered the labour market (between 1900 and 1940 the percentage of women employed outside the home increased by 23.5 per cent). The Women's Trade Union League (WTUL) was founded in 1903; and the militancy of women workers was increased and extended. But the existence of the WTUL was also indicative of the particularities of American political life: at the International Federation of Working Women's Convention in Vienna in 1923 there was a significant gap between the American group and their European counterparts:

Underlying the different points of view of the American and European working women on this proposal are their different conceptions of economics and social structure. American women have recognized the necessity for a woman movement within the labour movement; hence, the existence of the National Women's Trade Union League of America, an autonomous body working in co-operation with the American Federation of Labor, but specializing upon the problems of working women, which are admittedly different in any vital aspects from the problems of working men, and need to be emphasized by women in women's own way. The European labor movements, on the other hand, emphasize class-consciousness and deprecate a woman movement. Within their class European working women agree with European working men in this.[33].

Organized American feminism remained largely silent on the Wall Street crash, the rise of fascism at home and in Europe and the Depression.[34] Individual women, working in isolation, wrote about what they saw and how they felt about the poverty and despair in society at large, but their work remained obscure and had no significant impact. In much the same way, it is possible to see the same ahistorical, undialectical concept of feminism in the contemporary liberal women's movement. Hence some American femin-ists could welcome the election of Margaret Thatcher as British Prime Minister in 1979 regardless of her political views; and in the June 1980 issue of *MS* Gloria Steinem could interview Jihan Sadat in an article entitled 'Two cheers for Egypt', presenting the President's wife as a force for feminism in her country. One suspects that had it still been feasible, a similar piece on the Shah of Iran's wife might well have followed in the same pattern.

The fallacies of liberal feminism – whether that of the nineteenth or twentieth century – are all too easy to see. When Betty Friedan complains about the decline of the movement, she fails to see that her own ideological position has led her to the same state of impasse, and Zillah Eisenstein's advice to feminists to look at the mistakes of their predecessors is sound advice. But while we have been looking at the parallels between the two main feminist periods, it is important to note some of the differences, the greatest of which is probably the rise of mass-media feminism, of feminism as a saleable commodity on a vast scale.

The two most immediately obvious aspects of this phenomenon have been the emergence of what has been called the Women's Novel and the rise in the number of television series that show women in positions of authority and power, following the policy used since the late 1960s to show blacks in similar positions.

This kind of positive discrimination in terms of media images has an important function in liberal politics. Positive discrimination only goes so far, of course, and it can be argued that it merely preserves the status quo rather than challenging it, but there is no doubt that a whole new genre of very ambiguous television representations of women began to emerge in the 1970s and has proliferated in various ways.

TV 'feminism' offers two main types of New Woman: the active professional who holds her own in a male-dominated world, and the archetypal power-manipulator who controls her family with the same iron grip that she uses in her business affairs. Examples of the first type can be found in all kinds of American television programmes, from sitcoms to police series. In *Hill Street Blues*, for example, the Captain's lover is also his opponent in the courts, a beautiful but hard-nosed lawyer, given to defending criminals that he is trying to convict. In *Cagney and Lacey*, the protagonists are both women police-officers. When the series was tried out in a pilot film in 1981, *MS* ran an article on it, describing the way in which the traditional 'police buddies' formula was being regenerated by the use of women in the main roles, and discussing the 'feminization' of the executive producer who had previously worked on *Charlie's Angels*. It was also pointed out that the script-writing team at that time was exclusively female. The *MS* article argued that the film encountered special difficulties precisely because of the feminist content, because of the plot line that stresses the problems encountered by the women, with men reduced to supporting roles.

The 'feminism' of *Cagney and Lacey* is a good example of the problems presented by certain attitudes in the United States towards the women's movement in general. On the one hand, the series attempts to present an alternative image of women, it is written by women, with plots that stress the difficulties of professional women in combining careers and private lives (one police-officer married, with children, the other single, a combination which allows for various types of problem to be explored in different episodes). But the police system is still represented as the final source of order and good, and it is hard to understand what is feminist about the recruitment of women into a system of (patriarchal) control exercised by the state. With this inherent contradiction at the heart of the programme, it is small wonder that is so often slides into melodrama and sentimentality.

The image of the other type of 'liberated' woman can be found in the soap operas, in *Dynasty*, *Falcon Crest* and, to a lesser extent, *Dallas*. In all these series and their many spin-offs, women are predominantly sexual objects, who use their sexuality for their own ends. The wives and daughters who are denied public power resort to using sex as a way of establishing power in private. Those women who break the mould and run their own companies or private family empires are presented with considerable ambiguity – success in business usually means that they are portrayed as ruthless, bitchy, cruel and cold-hearted. It is notable that while the dull Blake Carrington in *Dynasty* controls his commercial empire and his wife Krystle with an iron hand, the viewers' sympathy remains with him. When Alexis Colby, his ex-wife, does exactly the same, she is the scheming villainess that everyone loves to hate in the true tradition of Hollywood melodrama. These images reinforce the stereotypes of man in command and woman in a subordinate role despite their apparent pretensions to the contrary.

The supposedly strong women of the television testify to the way in which the media has capitalized on the idea of woman as consumers. This trend can also be seen in the 'feminist' advertising campaigns, in which elegantly dressed businesswomen, obviously in positions of high authority, drink gin, fly TWA, smoke Gauloises and use simplified birth-control methods and panti-liners. This is the glossy woman's advertisement, matched step by step by the proliferation of small column advertisements for 'feminist products' – jewellery, running-shorts, vibrators, books, stickers, T-shirts ('Sexism is a social disease', 'Ladies Sewing Circle and Terrorist Society', 'Behind every successful woman is herself'), vaginal sponges, Susan B. Anthony pendants, shriek alarms, and non-sexist wedding-vow stationery, in short feminism as commerce. On the other hand, it could be argued that advertising campaigns and television series that feature women outside their traditional passive roles are inviting a rethinking of what feminism might mean. The liberal feminist platform defends the mass-media ventures on the ground that altering images can lead younger generations to question the rigidity of certain fixed social roles. The large market that has responded to the novels of writers like Erica Jong, Lisa Alther and Marilyn French is indicative, they would argue, of the groundswell of opinion that is demanding to see women in alternative roles.

But the question still remains as to how far it is possible to talk about the television series and the best-selling novel as being indicative of a feminist women's culture. Women have been getting together in groups for alternative living and working since the early 1960s, and a good deal of writing, craft work, film-making, theatre work, painting, sculpture etc. has been produced by such groups. What is often difficult to determine is the theoretical basis for such group ventures. If we consider one of the best-known projects, Judy Chicago's 'Dinner Party' exhibition, the absence of a theoretical basis becomes very apparent. Her project, which evolved into a nationally known venture, began as a collaboration between women volunteers and some 'feminist' men and attempted a revaluation of the contribution of women to history, in terms of their pro-duction of artefacts and their social and political roles. Starting with the assumption that ceramics and embroidery had traditionally been areas of women's work, Chicago and co-workers devised an exhibition that would put both areas of creativity into the limelight. They conceived of a gigantic three-sided dinner table, laid for thirty-nine guests, all famous women, and set upon a tiled floor bearing the names of 999 other women. Each place-setting had a specially designed embroidered runner and ceramic plate that symbolized the achievement of the particular guest. The result was stunningly beautiful, but begged as many questions as it raised. Chicago's denial of the value of embroidery and ceramics within the domestic context placed her squarely in the field of those who see achievement as measured by success in the male world. Hence an artist succeeds if her work is hung in a city museum and fails if it is hung on her living-room wall. Moreover, the choice of invitees reveals a startlingly historical sense. Women deemed to have been 'great' include not only the range of nineteenth-century American feminists, but women such as Elizabeth I, Eleanor of Aquitaine, St Bridget, Hatshepsut, Sacajawea, Caroline Herschel and Virginia Woolf. The criteria for 'greatness' are never adequately defined, and Chicago's guest list reads like the result of putting assorted well-known female names into a hat and selecting the first to come out. The 'Dinner Party' is beautiful to look at, and as such represents a great achievement for the team of artists who worked on it, but contributes nothing to the establishment of an alternative culture. Women are 'great' either because they achieved public recognition in a male world or because they did not and were thus undervalued, according to the way Chicago sees history. Her attitude is summed up in the book *The Dinner Party*, when she says that:

the china-painting world, and the household objects the women painted, seemed to be a perfect metaphor for women's domesticated and trivialized circumstances. It was an excruciating experience to watch enormously gifted women squander their creative talents on teacups.[35]

Other problems emerge from a consideration of another type of group project, such as Roberta Sklar's New York-based Women's Experimental Theatre company. Attempting to create a feminist theatre, with a feminist style of acting and a feminist form, Sklar turns to the idea of a closed theatre, in which the audience is a support group:

What we do in a real women's theatre can in no way be assessed, judged or accepted through a traditional analysis. Anyone looking at it from a traditional perspective isn't going to see. You need a new lens. The audience of women here has been learning to see together with us. Criticism in the press is meaningless, our constituency is not really represented there.[36]

The emphasis in Roberta Sklar's work is on establishing a sex-determined base for support and evaluation. The prime factor in the relationship between stage and audience becomes the commonality of sex, and in ideological terms this poses a good many problems. The fact of having a womb instead of a penis no more presupposes a unified concept of culture than vice versa. In her article 'Women and creativity: the demise of the dancing dog',[37] Cynthia Ozick discusses the absurdity of categorizing the artistic achievement of men and women according to biological criteria, arguing that genius is the property of both sexes alike and that 'a culture which does not allow itself to look clearly at the obvious through the universal accessibility of art is a culture of tragic delusion'. Ozick was writing in 1969, before the boom in women's studies that has since swept through the American educational system, but the questions she asks can be put equally to the perpetuators of a vision of history and creativity that excludes women and to those who seek to reverse the model and exclude men. A course on the women's novel, for example, that examines the work of women writers or a course on women in Shakespeare has no basis other than the arbitrary one of the biological determinant, and merely reiterates the assumptions of the male system. For example, if we take the 'hidden from history' idea that underlies a certain type of women's studies course, we can see that nothing fundamental is being challenged: a woman writer or artist, previously ignored, is revived, her work publicized, her achievement reclassified. But the result is to rearrange the system of priority evaluation in a given culture, not to rethink it. The notion of major and minor artists is the base that needs to be challenged, rather than the list of names. In short, a concept of women's studies that is not based on a radical restructuring of the existing notions of history only offers a semblance of change. As Charlotte Bunch has pointed out, the American system uses a policy of 'co-option' to absorb potentially dangerous thinking. It is the old colonial melting-pot theory, now being applied to feminism, and it means that what is presented publicly as a step forward for women goes no deeper than surface appearances. In 1946, Mary Beard raised precisely this point, in her book *Woman as Force in History*,[38] and although more recent feminist historians have criticized aspects of her work she was at least able to set out the problem coherently. Judy Chicago, Roberta Sklar, the thousands of women working and teaching in the belief that the creation of an alternative culture can take place within the mainstream of society, are on the road to ultimate absorption by that system because the fundamental language has remained unquestioned.

In looking at the difficulties of American feminism, it is all too easy to slip into the kind of disillusionment described by Betty Friedan and to see the women's movement as being in its terminal stages. But even though some of her misgivings may be valid, her negative analysis is fundamentally inadequate, based as it is on a liberal feminist perspective. As has been pointed out, there are very many voices of American feminism, and not all are silenced or muted in tone.

Attempts to 'feminize' the mass media may be doomed to failure, but there are women working in alternative groups, keeping well away from mass markets *because* of their belief in the need to restructure society. Likewise, amidst the plethora of intellectual women devising women's studies courses, there are those giving serious consideration to a theory of alternative culture, those questioning the viability of working within male-determined historiography, those examining the question of an alternative discourse. In 1974, in the first issue of *Quest*, Charlotte Bunch suggested that:

The primary goal is women gaining power in order to eliminate patriarchy and create a more humane society. We must determine what is necessary in order for women to obtain power and use it for these purposes. We must also look at the class, race, and sexual preference base of that power, if we are to create real change and not just acquire power for a few privileged women.

She goes on to outline five criteria for reform: (1) Does reform materially improve the lives of women, and, if so, which women and how many? (2) Does it build an individual woman's self-respect, strength and confidence? (3) Does it give women a sense of power, strength, and imagination as a group and help build structures for further change? (4) Does it educate women politically, enhancing their ability to criticize and challenge the system in the future? (5) Does it weaken patriarchal control of society's institutions and help women gain power over them?

Radicals like Charlotte Bunch warn that change is part of a process and that the process must be underpinned by a sound theoretical base, otherwise male pin-ups, open marriage, gay liberation ear-rings, courses on undiscovered women poets, the ordination of female bishops and the election of the first woman President will be construed as feminist advances. The very term 'feminist' has become virtually meaningless in the American context and perhaps the time has come to dispense with it altogether, she argues.

There has never been a single voice of American feminism. But what has begun to happen now is that the many varied voices are blending together in opposition to the Moral Majority campaigners, trying to formulate a coherent defence. Instead of voices crying out in protest and formulating strategies for social change, what we have now is the muted tone of self-preservation.

But in private, out of the reach of NOW, *MS* and the many liberal voices, questions are being asked within individual communities. In the same way that some radical theatre groups moved out of the cities in the 1970s to live and work in new organizational structures, so one line of the American women's movement has followed that same path. Asked to give her views on the feminist future in the year 2000 in *MS*, February 1981, Phyllis Birkby, a California-based architect, did not talk about the need for reassessment and a new humility, as did some of the other women interviewed. Instead, she discussed briefly the need for a restructuring of the physical environment in which people live, a restructuring that would involve radical ideological changes at its centre:

We need a whole new matrix. But in the past 10 years, we have made some hopeful beginnings. I am encouraged by the revival of midwifery and creation of birthing centres; the growing militance of the disabled providing a greater mobility for pregnant women and young children; 'inclusionary' mixed-use zoning in some cities; more women's centers, bookstores, shelters, coffee-houses, and cultural centers; the networking efforts of the Women's School of Planning and Architecture, which looks at new ways of integrating housing with economic opportunity for women. These are all building blocks that may become a new matrix of connections.

Long-range future planning is then perhaps the real contribution that the American women's movement has to offer. Significantly, there has been an increase in the number of women writing science fiction, and within that genre the emphasis has been on the problems of alternative social organization. The single, dominant hero figure is often replaced by the group or by the hero–apprentice pair. The cynic might argue that women are merely retreading the path of Utopian socialism, but no social revolution has ever been founded on cynicism. If we look beyond the exaggerated claims for the advancement of women in the

United States through tokenism, on the one hand, and the sense of failure that some American feminists feel because the desired changes have failed to materialize, on the other hand, the tiny American socialist-ecological group can be seen as a most hopeful signpost to the future.

Finally, of course, we should not underestimate the tradition of American optimism, so often dismissed as naïve by Europeans. Discussing the failure of the ERA ratification campaign, Gloria Steinem chose to frame the negative within what she claimed was a context of growing anger on the part of women against repressive government attitudes. The piece was entitled 'Post ERA politics: losing a battle but winning a war?[39] In it Steinem argued, somewhat ruefully, that whereas race was a clear-cut election issue, sex was still a debatable one, and she urged women to organize themselves, to plan campaigns *and* to consider the needs of the voters. This first, still slightly vague, assumption suggests that the next phase of American feminism will be based at grass-roots level, now that the time of vast generalizations about total change is well and truly over. Moreover, the way in which the new Right has forced a link between women's issues and welfare issues may be turned to advantage, as women become more involved in programmes of social reform and leave behind the 'great female individual' image of the 1970s American feminist, rooted as she was in the nineteenth-century liberal tradition of middle-class élitism.

What is firmly in the past is the strident voice of American feminism that was so strenuously hyped by the media in the late 1960s and early 1970s. That phase, which was undoubtedly beneficial to embryonic women's movements in many parts of the world, is now over, and the way forward for American feminism would seem to lie in a return to grass roots, away from internationalism.

Notes

1 B. Friedan, *The Second Stage* (New York: Summit, 1981).

2 Quoted in B. Roszak and T. Roszak, *Masculine/Feminine: Readings in Sexual Mythology and the Liberation of Women* (New York: Harper & Row, 1969), p. 163.

3 Quoted in R. Morgan, *Sisterhood is Powerful* (New York: Vintage Books, 1970) p. 585.

4 Quoted in Roszak and Roszak, *Masculine/Feminine*, p. 27.

5 For a full account of Lenin and Zetkin's discussions of women's issues, see V. I. Lenin and K. Zetkin, *On the Emancipation of Women* (Moscow: Progress Publishers, 1938).

6 M. Dixon. 'The rise of women's liberation', *Ramparts*, vol. 8, no. 6 (1969), p. 57.

7 J. Hole and E. Levine, *Rebirth of Feminism* (New York: Quadrangle, 1971) p. 148.

8 Quoted in Hole and Levine, *Rebirth*, p. 128.

9 Quoted in Hole and Levine, *Rebirth*, pp. 259–60.

10 S. Firestone, *The Dialectic of Sex: The Case for Feminist Revolution* (London: Cape, 1971) p. 111.

11 C. Bunch, 'Beyond either/or: feminist options', *Quest: A Feminist Quarterly*, vol. 3, no. 1 (1976).

12 M. Daly, *Gyn/Ecology* (Boston, Mass.: Beacon, 1978) pp. 423–40.

13 J. Parvati, *Hygieia: A Woman's Herbal* (New York: Wildwood House, 1978).

14 *MS*, December 1981.

15 Quoted in Roszak and Roszak, *Masculine/Feminine*, p. 274.

16 Morgan, *Sisterhood*, p. xxxviii.

17 Quoted in Hole and Levine, *Rebirth*, p: 85.

18 The Bill of Rights called for:

    I Equal Rights Constitutional Amendment

    II Enforcement of Laws Banning Sex Discrimination in Employment

    III Maternity Leave Rights in Employment and in Social Security Benefits

    IV Tax Deduction for Home and Child Care Expenses for Working Parents

    V Child Care Centres

    VI Equal and Unsegregated Education

    VII Equal Job Training Opportunities and Allowance for Women in Poverty

    VIII The Right of Women to Control their Reproductive Lives.

19 Quoted in Hole and Levine, Rebirth, p. 145.

20 For a general view of Schlafly's anti-feminist stance, see P. Schlafly, *Power of the Positive Women* (New York: Jove, 1981).

21 Z. Eisenstein, *The Radical Future of Liberal Feminism* (New York and London: Longman, 1981) p. 235.

22 Eisenstein, *Radical Future,* p. 236.

23 E. C. Stanton, S. B. Anthony, M. J. Gage and I. H. Harper (eds), *History of Woman Suffrage,* 6 vols (first published 1881–1922; republished New York: Arno Press and *New York Times,* 1969).

24 A. Rossi (ed), *The Feminist Papers* (New York: Bantam, 1973), p. 248.

25 *Dial,* vol. 4, no. 1 (1843). Quoted in M. Fuller, *Woman in the Nineteenth Century* (New York: Norton, 1971), p. 115.

26 S. Grimke, 'Letters on the equality of the sexes', in Rossi, *Feminist Papers*, p. 315.

27 E. C. Stanton in a paper submitted to the hearing of the House Committee on the Judiciary in 1896. For a full discussion of this issue, see A. Kraditor, *'The new immigration and labor'* in *The Ideas of the Woman Suffrage Movement 1890–1920* (New York: Double-day, 1971), pp. 105–37.

28 Quoted in E. Flexner, *Century of Struggle* (Cambridge, Mass: Harvard University Press, 1959), p. 90.

29 D. Brown, *Women of the Wild West* (London and Sydney: Pan, 1975 [1958]). First published in Great Britain as *The Gentle Tamers* (London: Barrie and Jenkins, 1973).

30 B. Fisher-Manick, 'Race and class: beyond personal politics', *Quest: A Feminist Quarterly,* vol. 3, no. 4 (1977), pp. 2–15.

31 Quoted in L. W. Banner, *Women in Modern America: A Brief History* (New York: Harper & Row, Colophon Books, 1974), p. 13.

32 A. K. Schulman (ed), *Red Emma Speaks: Selected Writings and Speeches by Emma Goldman* (New York: Vintage, 1972), p. 134.

33 For a comparative perspective on European and American working women's organizations, see R. J. Evans, 'Socialists and revolution-aries' in *The Feminists* (London: Croom Helm, 1977), pp. 144–88.

34 Though Susan Ware, in her book *Beyond Suffrage: Women in the New Deal* (Cambridge, Mass., and London: Harvard University Press, 1981), does quote Eleanor Roosevelt and her circle as being aware of the implications of fascist ideology for women.

35 J. Chicago, *The Dinner Party* (New York: Doubleday, 1980), p. 11.

36 C. Brunner and R. Sklar, 'Toward creating a women's theatre', *Drama Review,* vol. 24, no. 2 (1980), pp 23–41.

37 C. Ozick, 'Women and creativity: the demise of the dancing dog' in

V. Gornick and B. K. Moran (eds) *Woman in Sexist Society: Studies in Power and Powerlessness* (New York: Basic, 1971).

38 M. Beard, *Woman as Force in History* (New York: Collier Macmillan, 1946).

39 G. Steinem, 'Post ERA politics: losing a battle but winning the war?', *MS*, vol. 11, no. 7 (1983).

Chapter Two

The German Democratic Republic

Any discussion of the status and role of women in the GDR must be approached through one piece of simple statistical evidence: the fact that by the early 1980s some 87 per cent of all women of working age were either studying or employed. For such a high percentage of women to be actively involved in the workforce, there clearly has had to be a back-up system of social services, particularly with regard to maternity leave and child care, and evidence of such social services is easy enough to see. Maternity leave extends six weeks before childbirth and twenty weeks afterwards, with maternity allowances equivalent to net average earnings payable during that period. A birth allowance of approximately £250 is payable for every child born, and mothers are entitled to the *Babyjahr*, a minimum of twelve months' leave from work with the job guaranteed at the end of that period. Support for single mothers is more extensive, with additional child benefits and priority for crèche places given. Crèches may be organized on a local community basis or within the place of work (factories tend to have their own crèche systems, for example), and 1981 figures showed that, out of every 1,000 children under the age of three, 612 were placed in one kind of crèche or another. Children begin to attend school at the age of 6 (kindergarten classes are from the age of 3 to 6, and each local school has after-hours play facilities for children awaiting collection by parents).[1]

Such social services stand in stark contrast to the equivalent facilities available in Britain, France, or the United States, and demands for more extensive child-care facilities have been a central plank of the women's movement in Western countries since the early 1970s, together with the demand for more liberal abortion and family laws. Abortion (but only up to the twelfth week) has been allowed on demand in the GDR since 1972, and a system of no-fault divorce operates, with an interesting three-quarters of all petitions being brought by women. There is a wide network of family-planning clinics and marriage guidance centres; and, in an effort to liberate women from the duties of unpaid and unrecognized nursing of the elderly and handicapped, there are community networks of state and voluntary home-help aid schemes. Holiday schemes are run through trade unions, organized once again on a community basis, assuring annual holidays at home and abroad (with the Black Sea coastal resorts being popular favourites) to those categories of the population that would be defined as underprivileged in the West.

The social advantages of such welfare structures are undeniable and outweigh the voices of criticism raised both within the GDR and, more particularly, by Western journalists with an anti-socialist axe to grind. Certainly there is a case to be made against the restriction of abortion to twelve weeks only, just as there is a case to be made against the long hours that very young children spend in crèches (many open at 6 a.m. and some insist that children have to be brought in at that time in order to organize the day's activities on the same basis for all comers). The rising birth rate can no doubt be linked to the improved leave facilities for working mothers, especially the *Babyjahr*, and cynics may claim that this step forward marks less an advance for women's needs than an attempt to persuade the female population to produce more children. But regardless of the quibbles – though the quibbles should not by any means be ignored – it should be plain that women in the GDR enjoy and perceive as basic rights what women in the West view as an impossible dream. An East German woman friend – not even a party member – who spent some months recently in London and Paris, commented favourably on a great deal that she found helpful in Western feminist writing, but remarked that she wondered how those of us with families managed, since we were forced to live with such inadequate child-care and welfare facilities. It was pointed out to her that since she had mixed exclusively in intellectual and artistic circles, the facilities she perceived as appalling were actually the best available. Only the privileged few at the tip of the British iceberg can afford to pay a third of their salaries for child care and, as women, receive no income-tax relief on the sum they pay. The options for most British women are far less congenial. Compared with what is available in Britain, the facilities in the GDR can only be admired and envied.

Moreover, the high percentage of women in the overall workforce has led to a shift in attitude towards women's role in society. As in the USSR, the medical profession is dominated by women, whilst women account for 50 per cent of all judges and 50 per cent of the total trade union membership. Care is taken in school textbooks to avoid sexist role definitions – early reading schemes, for example, show mothers at work, with fathers looking after children and doing housework. During my time in the GDR, I have met women in all kinds of positions in authority – directing factories and coal-mines, organizing trade unions, running cities – and neither being seen nor seeing themselves as unusual. For example, the *Oberbürgermeisterin* (Mayor) of Dessau, a large industrial city south-west of Berlin, is a woman from a working-class background whose career can

in many respects be said to typify the progress of professional upward mobility of a woman of her age. Born in 1932
she attended a local school, worked in a shoe factory and
then, through the further-education classes available to
factory workers, moved on eventually in the early 1950s to
study economics and local government in Berlin. In 1957
she was elected to the local planning committee in Dessau,
a position of some significance since 80 per cent of the city
had been destroyed in the Second World War. Finally, in
1963, she was elected mayor and has remained in office
ever since. Two of her three children were born after her
election.

So what, one might ask, does this biography prove?
That some women attain public office from time to time is
a recognized fact, with the British Prime Minister Margaret
Thatcher as a prime example. Yet what seems to be significant about the Mayor of Dessau's case is precisely what
differentiates her most strikingly from Margaret Thatcher,
whose wealthy marriage gave her the power to employ
nannies, cooks and cleaners and concentrate on her public
affairs. The Mayor of Dessau comes from a working-class
background, spent her childhood in the period of Hitler's
supremacy, and yet perceives early deprivation as a con-
tributory factor in her present success: 'Perhaps I had it
easier than a middle-class girl because I had to stand on my
own feet sooner and that helped me through the bad
years.'[2] Once involved in the trade union movement and
later in student politics, she campaigned strongly for crèche
facilities. As mayor she points with pride to the crèche and
kindergarten facilities available in Dessau, stressing that
they are better than in many other towns. She has also
campaigned for reduced hours for nursing mothers and
established a local home laundry service. Throughout her
career she has taken her children to council meetings.

In the West, the Mayor of Dessau could be described as a
feminist. She has balanced motherhood and a career, has

been aware of the specific problems of women, has striven to set up a local welfare system that even helps families solve the problem of the weekly wash, and this in spite of her origins in rural peasant society in Nazi Germany, where a woman's place was rigidly circumscribed. Nor is her story particularly unusual. She is merely one of a whole generation of women for whom the advent of socialism meant a total restructuring of their social expectations and un-dreamed-of class mobility. Yet, again in common with the majority of successful women in the GDR, not only would she not describe herself as a feminist, but she would also strongly reject any attempt to pin such a description on her.

The rejection of what is described as 'bourgeois' or 'capitalist' feminism is widespread, both by trade unionists and by intellectuals and writers. This fact has created problems for Western feminists when they are faced with obvious advances women in the GDR have made over the past thirty years. East German women appear to have gained ground that in Western societies still forms the basis of feminist demands, yet there remain glaring examples of overt sexist discrimination that Western feminism would find intolerable. Children's toys, for example, are marketed along divisively sex-biased lines, with dolls for girls and trucks and toy soldiers for boys. The queues in the supermarkets are mainly female, with the occasional man under 30 here and there in the crowd. Official information booklets inexorably link *die Frau* with *die Familie*. In the centre of Berlin, the Museum of German History stresses the achievements of men to such an extent that in the section dedicated to post-Second World War history a visitor might be forgiven if she assumed that women had played almost no role at all in the formation of the new state, even though everyone knows that the actual physical task of clearing the rubble and rebuilding the ravaged cities was largely carried out by women. Western feminists must feel uneasy at such apparent contradictions and question whether women in the GDR have in fact come very much further than anyone else. At the same time, East German women view with deep suspicion what they perceive as over-emphasis on 'trivia' at the expense of tackling fundamental problems, and this has become their essential criticism of Western women's movements. 'Why waste time discussing sexuality when there are so many practical problems to be solved?' was a common question to me, from young and old women alike. Dr Horz, Professor of Ethics at Humboldt University, first vice-president of the UNESCO Women's Committee, co-ordinator of the 1979 Copenhagen Women's Conference, has sharp criticism for what she perceives as the Anglo-American involvement in 'non-rational problems'. Opposed to any theory approaching biologism, she insists that the case for a specificity of female experience is sociologically determined. The gulf between her and Betty Friedan is as wide as that between Christabel Pankhurst and Clara Zetkin might have been.

The general rationalization of the rejection of so-called bourgeois feminism derives in part from a certain sense of complacency, based on a belief that the oppression of women is directly linked to capitalism and is therefore not problematic within a socialist state. Nevertheless, the discussion of the link between capitalism and patriarchy that has long dominated Western feminism has begun to emerge in the GDR too. If, as was traditionally accepted, patriarchy and capitalism go hand in hand, what are we to make of the residual patriarchal attitudes extant in socialist society, attitudes that can be seen most clearly where issues of women's sexuality are concerned? The relationship between feminist concerns and Marxist revolutionary society is very complex, and deserves much closer attention than it has hitherto received. Western detractors of the GDR are all too prompt to attack the apparent lack of a publicly defined women's movement similar to those in the West, whilst within the GDR there is a tendency to over-simplify and trivialize those movements in other countries which are striving for greater emancipation of women. Barbara Einhorn has analyzed what she perceives as the contradictory attitudes both within the GDR and about the GDR over feminist issues, and points out that whilst those contradictions are being expressed in the media and literature of the GDR, they do not 'have their parallel in the growth of a grass roots women's organization as has been the case in the West'.[3]

There is, of course, no women's movement as such in the GDR. There are women's organizations within trade unions and there is the national Demokratischer Frauenbund Deutschlands (DFD) which was founded in 1947 and arose out of the union of anti-fascist women's committees and women workers' groups. The interesting point about this organization is the age range of its members, for although all women over the age of 18 are eligible to join, over 65 per cent are under 35. There is no written documentation of the causes of this tendency. but after I had had lengthy talks with the chairwoman several factors began to emerge. The first was the intensity of the GDR's attempts to involve women in the workforce, not only at the level of unskilled workers but increasingly at higher levels. It was pointed out that whereas in 1970 only 28 per cent of women had obtained their skilled workers' certificate, ten years later that figure had increased to 55 per cent, with an astonishing 86 per cent of women agricultural workers having acquired qualifications. But what seems to have happened is that an older generation of women has not made the adjustment to a sense of socialist sisterhood, thus the tradition with regard to the role a woman is expected to play both inside and outside the home that divides GDR society in a very striking way has been maintained. In the new postwar society, women were expected to leap out of their homes into the public arena, and this after years of relegation to an idealized second-class status under Nazism. The result of such a precipitous step seems only to be beginning to be felt now, with signs of an identity crisis among women beginning to show in a variety of ways.

In her book, *The Nazi Organization of Women*, Jill Stephenson discusses the inherent contradictions in the Nazi policy towards women. On the one hand, there was a clear rejection of women's involvement in conventional political activity, with women being relegated to the home, away from the unsavoury activities of professional politicians. On the other hand, from 1933 onwards, there was some anxiety about the need to make women more politically aware, and Stephenson suggests that in fact women were 'peculiarly resistant to National Socialism' on the whole, probably because of the power of religion.[4] She quotes an extract from the *Volkischer Beobachter*, the official Nazi newspaper, of September 1935, in which women are urged to become aware of the tasks awaiting them as women, though clearly not as feminists:

We claim no rights for our sex such as that woman politician [Rosa Luxembourg] demanded . . . Rather we want to fulfil the tasks which the nation sets us as women . . . What we are striving for today is a completely different kind of politicization of women, it is the dedication of women to the nation and therefore to the state, which is organically constructed upon the reality of race and nation.[5]

The fundamental fascist dichotomy between woman as an idealized image and woman's place in the social hierarchy is summed up by Jill Stephenson in a few words:

It was partly Hitler's personal attachment to the image of women as 'mothers of the nation' which delayed and then vitiated the introduction of labour conscription for women during the Second World War, although in his *Gotterdämmerung* mentality early in 1945 he was prepared to see women enlisted as soldiers and sent to the front.[6]

The advent of National Socialism wiped out the few steps towards female emancipation that had been taken during the previous fifty years. German women had acquired the right to vote in 1918, after a lengthy suffrage campaign involving, as had the American and British campaigns, both liberal and socialist feminists predominantly from the middle classes. But even before Hitler's rise to power, German feminism had begun to disintegrate, in spite of the fact that the German Social Democratic Women's Movement, under the leadership of Clara Zetkin, was probably the most impressive socialist women's organization in the early years of the century. August Bebel, the leader of the Social Democrats until 1913, was the author of one of the earliest and most significant works on socialist feminism, *Woman Under Socialism*, first published in 1883.

The SPD (Sozialdemokratische Parte Deutschlands) women's movement organized an International Socialist Women's Conference in Stuttgart. At this conference two basic principles were endorsed: a commitment to suffrage for men and women, and no co-operation with bourgeois feminists. But one year later, in 1908, Clara Zetkin was replaced as leader of the women's movement by Luise Zietz, a far less radical woman, and in the same year German feminism took a further step to the Right when the reactionary German-Evangelical Women's League joined the Federation of German Women's Associations and defeated a proposal in the general assembly to legalize abortion. Abortion, together with contraception, never found universal support, even amongst the SPD women's movement and it was a relatively easy step to move from an anti-abortion platform to an advocation of enforced sterilization for unsuitable social elements, a policy that the Federation of German Women's Associations began to discuss after the First World War. In spite of the principles of the 1908 conference, bourgeois feminism ousted radical women and began to concentrate increasingly on the 'moral role' of women in German society, campaigning for increased censorship and declaring motherhood and housekeeping to be the proper roles for women. Hitler's brand of anti-feminism had many women as supporters, even before the National Socialists came to power.

With this kind of history, it is hardly surprising that East German women today are suspicious of any concept of feminism that is not firmly rooted in socialism. They have learned from what Jean Quataert has called 'the uneasy alliance of unequal partners' (the partners being women and the working class in imperial Germany).[7] But Bebel's equation of women and slaves as equal in oppression, while serving its purpose in an emergent revolutionary context, has to be looked at differently inside a socialist society where supposedly all forms of oppression are being overcome. And, as Western Marxist feminists have so often pointed out, while one kind of oppression can be explained in class terms, it is impossible to consider women in those same terms. Hence the emergence of the idea of the 'woman question', the problem very much *with* a name, but without any clear solution.

In 1918, at the first All-Russian Women's Congress, Lenin had this to say about housework:

Notwithstanding all the liberating laws that have been passed, woman continues to be a domestic slave, because petty housework crushes, strangles, stultifies and degrades her, chains her to the kitchen and the nursery, and wastes her labour on barbarously unproductive, petty, nerve-wracking drudgery. The real emancipation of women, real communism, will begin only when a mass struggle (led by the proleteriat in power) is started against this petty domestic economy . . . Do we devote sufficient attention to this question which, theoretically, is indisputable for every communist? Of course not . . . [8]

The problem of housework remains a thorn in the side of women in the GDR. The need for women to enter the labour force outside the home has led to the development of child-care services and systems of benefits, but at the same time little or nothing seems to have been done to tackle the whole question of whether housework holds the same status as paid work outside the home. Indeed, a conclusion that can be drawn from the absence of debate on the housework issue would seem to be that it has not been taken very much further than Lenin's initial statement. Moreover, the high cost of labour-saving devices within the home (compared with in the West) means that not all women by any means have the advantages of washing-machines, refrigerators, driers, etc., even though they may still have all the chores to do when they get home after a day's work, and not all city mayors are as enlightened and as aware of the problems as the Mayor of Dessau with her home laundry service project. So the problem remains unsolved, both on the practical level, with East German women still taking on the tasks of housework in addition to their paid employment, helped occasionally by husbands, and on the theoretical level, with the fundamental issue of the relationship between production and reproduction still undiscussed.

Linked to the whole question of housework is the question of marriage and the family. I was interested to see how the word *Familie* was so frequently linked to *Frau*, and when on occasion I queried this and suggested that this terminological link-up had sexist implications, the responses varied from bewilderment to hostility. Clearly, the argument went, the link-up was primarily between women and the family, because the women give birth to the children. Pushing further, I suggested that this was a biologist line of argument, and pointed out that Western women were continually debating the problem of how to restructure the traditional family unit and reallocate the power base between parents or parent figures. But although I have discussed this question with substantial numbers of women in the GDR, over several years, I cannot find any evidence that the problem is being seriously considered – except, as I hope to show in the following pages, by some of the new women writers.

I have never been entirely satisfied with my discussions about socialist marriage either. On the one hand, everyone is quite clear that marriage has ceased to be primarily a property transaction, as it remains in the West. The divorce rate in the GDR is extremely high, with women bringing three-quarters of all the petitions, and with working-class women divorcing as readily as their middle-class sisters. No-fault divorce, by simple agreement between both parties, is the norm, but when I talked to women who had been through the process once or twice it was clear that they divorced for reasons that could be clearly indentified – violence, drunkenness, incompatibility. The availability of subsidized housing together with the widespread system of crèches lead to a large number of young marriages, which in turn results in a high percentage of youthful divorce. Where children are concerned, the mother usually gets custody, which is to be expected given the insistence on the relationship between mothers and children; and child maintenance is then deducted from salary at source, so the problem of fathers not keeping up their maintenance payments does not arise. Maintenance is defined as a moral responsibility on the part of the parent and is definitely not perceived as a relic of a capitalist society in which property serves as the basis for marriage.

Divorce, then, is a straightforward procedure. Single parents receive preferential treatment regarding housing and crèche places, and there is no social stigma attached to illegitimacy or living alone. Yet, as one might expect, the process of divorce is painful and often humiliating, and on the one occasion when I sat in court to witness a divorce hearing, the distress of the couple was plain to see. Why, then, in a society that has removed the social stigma of living together – German, unlike English, actually has a term for the partner one lives with – and which has removed the property base of marriage, do people still bother to get married at all, and in such large numbers too? This is a question to which I have never received an answer that makes coherent sense. One young trade unionist told me that she believed marriage held a different meaning in a socialist society, but when pressed to define that changed meaning could only come up with the notion that marriage is a public statement of greater security within a relationship, which still attributes a high status to the institution of marriage. Jutta Gisi, a sociologist at the Berlin Academy, studying women and the family, offered other suggestions. She pointed out that marriage was a calculable factor in the planning of a new society, with regard to building programmes, to take just one example, and that therefore it was in the state's interest, at least in the initial stages, to encourage marriage. The GDR, moreover, with its massive underpopulation problem after 1946 had to embark on a propaganda campaign to encourage women to produce more children, while at the same time encouraging them to continue working outside the home. She admitted that, ideologically, marriage still presented a problem in the GDR, but argued that, nevertheless, the concept of socialist marriage as a public statement of a union between two partners equally defined under the law differed radically from the capitalist concept of marriage. In capitalist societies, she believes, marriage acts as a safety-valve – men take their problems into the marriage relationship and hold the power within the household. The utilization of the family as a power base for individual men acts as a distraction from the real business of co-operating with women in the struggle to build a redefined social order. Jutta Gisi's view makes sense, in absolute terms, but still does not explain the apparent lack of any anti-marriage voices. Clearly marriage is a sign of something that cannot be explained in purely sociological terms. Based on a belief in the values of monogamy, it has come to be seen as a sign of ideal order, in which the harmony between two individuals mirrors the harmony of the state – except that so many of these ideal visions end in the divorce court.

The divorce hearing I attended was a fairly typical one. A couple in their early twenties, married as students, claimed that the marriage had irretrievably broken down. Interestingly, her reasons differed radically from his. She wanted it all over quickly; she had grown apart from him in the few years they had been together and had initiated the proceedings. Asked a series of questions by the judge (a woman) she pointed out that there were no other people involved, but that she no longer loved him and felt that their interests had diverged to the point at which they had nothing to say to each other any more. 'I think it was a stupid thing to do to get married at 18,' was her comment. He, on the other hand, took a different line. He had agreed to the divorce but was unhappy about it, because he still loved her and wanted her back. He suggested that she had not tried hard enough to save the marriage and implied that he had behaved with greater maturity over the whole affair. In the final stages of the marriage, he had made her give up her key to their flat, and he told the court that she refused to account for herself and that he could not accept her coming in and out whenever she felt like it. She saw this as patronizing and unacceptable in the extreme.

What I found interesting about this case was the way in which the couple fell into stereotyped patterns of behaviour. He patronized her, she burst into tears and protested against being treated as a child. Her case for the breakdown of the relationship through her own growth came across badly compared with his insistence on his continued love for her, opposed to her wilfulness. Although the judge accepted the petition, asking for a few days to sort out financial details of the settlement and ordering that the key must be returned to the wife immediately, I was left with the feeling that what was entirely missing was an awareness of the woman's case. If there is one thing the women's movements in the West have managed to accomplish, it is to introduce a new terminology, a new discourse, in which the problem of different patterns of personal development within a relationship is recognized as a feminist issue.

That it should be a woman who claimed to have changed and developed faster than her husband is also interestingly typical of social patterns in the GDR. The availability of training courses through the trade unions, the huge increase in the number of working men and women from traditionally non-intellectual backgrounds who now receive higher education, indeed the whole emphasis on education and acquisition of specialist skills, has resulted in greater mobility for women within the labour force at all levels. And although the numbers of women in central government and in senior positions nationally are lower than might be expected, there has certainly been a huge increase in the numbers of women in the professions and in skilled manufacturing work. In this the GDR is in the special position of having Turkish guest workers perform the more menial tasks which in the USSR, for example, are carried out by women. An East German joke about Russian women bitterly notes that they are the USSR's *Gastarbeiterinnen*, or immigrant workers. By not filling all the most menial positions with women, and by making available training courses for skilled workers, the GDR has ensured that the standard of achievement by women in the workforce is one of the highest in eastern Europe.

But even while East German women seem to be achieving so much in material terms, some have already begun to ask more fundamental questions, for example, the question whether women's needs and desires are not fundamentally different from those of their male comrades. Reviewing[9] the book that might be described as the first popular feminist book to appear in the GDR, Maxie Wander's *Guten Morgen, du Schöne* ('Good Morning, Beautiful'),[10] one of the GDR's leading writers, Christa Wolf, asks whether women ought to aspire to enter the male-dominated rat race that operates hierarchically, whether they ought to want 'to take on roles that have done such damage to men throughout the ages'.[11] Here then is a woman writing about the work of another woman and raising the whole question of whether women's goals differ from those of men. Beneath Christa Wolf's overt question lies the more profound one: where from within socialism will the impulse come for a new social order, an order that will not so much seek to spread the problems around between the sexes but will be a true alternative? It is tempting to recall the protest by 30,000 women at Greenham Common in December 1982, angered and frustrated by the war rhetoric of the Conservative government and by the plans to establish cruise missile bases on British soil. The women of Greenham Common, whilst making a humanitarian protest for peace, nevertheless did not invite men to join that protest, precisely because of the centuries of men's involvement with the machinery of war-making. Christa Wolf's point about those roles which have done damage to men throughout the ages can be seen at its clearest if we consider the state apparatus of armies, the male structure *par excellence.*

Christa Wolf's questions are not asked in a vacuum, but are designed to focus the reader's attention on Maxie Wander's book. When *Guten Morgen, du Schöne* came out in 1977, just a few months before the author's death from cancer that is so movingly documented in her 'Diary and Letters',[12] it proved a phenomenal success. The book caught the public imagination and became an instant best seller, both in the GDR and in the Federal Republic, and parts of the text were then transferred to the stage, playing to packed houses for several years. Precisely why the book struck such a chord is difficult to determine, but what its success does indicate is the interest aroused by the presentation of women's experiences and women's opinions, for it is a book in which women's voices are heard speaking directly to the reader. Maxie Wander interviews nineteen women, and the book is the transcript of what those women have to say. Ruth, the 22-year-old waitress, Lena, the 43-year-old teacher, Gabi, the 16-year-old schoolgirl, all speak through the pages of the book, telling us about their lives, their hopes and fears, their happiness and frustrations, and through this collection of monologues we build up a composite picture of the life of women in the GDR.

The idea of interviewing women with a view to producing a book about women was not new. In 1974, Sarah Kirsch published her collection of tape-recorded interviews, *Die Pantherfrau: Fünf Unfrisierte Erzählungen aus dem Kassettenrecorder* ('Panther Women: Five Undoctored Stories out of a Tape Recorder').[13] Earlier, in the Federal Republic, Erika Runge's book of interviews of seventeen women, *Frauen: Versuche zur Emanzipation* ('Women: An Attempt at Emancipation'), had been published in 1970,[14] but there are fundamental differences between Maxie Wander's book and the earlier collections of interviews. Whereas Erika Runge's book has a precise aim, that of determining the level of emancipation among women in German society, and Sarah Kirsch's book is devised as a montage, with the tape recorder being used for greater realism, Maxie Wander's technique is to allow the women total freedom of expression, to allow them to write the book with their own words. The voices we hear are not muted by any authorial intervention, and the expressions of bewilderment, dissatisfaction and yet, at the same time, of hope are what give the book such power and authenticity. Maxie Wander herself claimed that she did not set out to create any kind of representative picture of East German women, but simply wanted to create a situation in which women could talk honestly about themselves, in which they could admit to the kind of fears that Ruth acknowledges when she says: 'I think my problem is this: I'm living at a time when there are lots of possibilities for women, and I'm a coward.'[15]

Maxie Wander's book is not self-consciously feminist and yet it is impossible to read it without making connections with the kind of writing by women that has been emerging in Western countries since the late 1960s. Like many of the current French writers she deliberately blurs the line between fiction and documentary, and like many English and American women writers she is interested in letting her material shape itself, letting her characters take the power into their own hands. Moreover, the kind of conversations that lie behind the monologues, and the process whereby Maxie Wander obviously managed to create a relationship with other women that would allow such openness, would seem to have much in common with the consciousness-raising group sessions which have been so much a part of Western feminism. In talking with such intensity about personal experiences, the speakers open the way for other women to share those experiences, to compare their own lives with those of others, in short, to communicate on a large scale. In addition, Maxie Wander's book deconstructs the author, opens up a channel between the readers, whether men or women, and the speakers in the book itself, in which the author's role is that of the agent who enables this meeting to take place rather than the mastermind who guides us all through it.

Although *Guten Morgen, du Schöne* has been an outstanding success, Maxie Wander is by no means the only woman to attempt to create a new kind of writing. The new literature that has emerged since the founding of the GDR is virtually dominated by women prose writers. Drama and poetry do not seem to be the prime media through which East German women express themselves at present, but as prose writers they are probably more prolific than women in any other European society. The *grande dame* of East German writers is Anna Seghers, a realist novelist of extraordinary power whose stories so often focus on the pain and suffering of women caught up in the maelstrom of world events. In an essay on a meeting with Anna Seghers, Christa Wolf pinpoints her technique in a telling little anecdote:

It often seems as if she is only satisfied when she discovers the opposite in something that appears quite clear and easy to explain, the comic in the tragic, a spark of pity in evil, an ounce of selfishness in the good, the profane in the excessively noble, the useful spot of doubt in the indubitable. In Moscow with a delegation, she gets back late for lunch at the hotel. She has been in GUM, the big store on the Red Square, she says. She eats her soup in silence, but her thoughts are busy. Finally it has to come out: Look, do you suppose Marx knew that? – Knew what, Anna? – Well, how many blouses this huge country needs. They've just delivered mountains of blouses to GUM . . . [16]

Significantly, this anecdote relates a conversation between two women about an issue of direct relevance to women. In another interview recorded in the same essay, Anna Seghers tells how she received a letter from a woman who had undergone the same tragic experiences as a character in one of her novels, and who wrote to say she was certain that Seghers had used her life story as a model. In telling this story, she illustrates another dimension of the process of creating 'realist' fiction, the point at which life itself follows the patterns the fiction writer has herself invented.

In 1977 Patricia Herminghouse published an article on East German women writers in a West German book on literature in the GDR. Her chapter was called 'Wunschbild, Vorbild oder Porträt? Zur Darstellung der Frau im Roman der DDR' ('Ideal, model or portrait? On the representation of women in the novel of the GDR').[17] Herminghouse attempts to explain the phenomenon of women writers by documenting the changes in prose style and drawing certain conclusions. She divides the East German women's novel into three phases: the *Aufbauroman*, or building novel, the *Ankunftsroman*, or arrival novel, and the *verändertesbewusstseinsroman* or changing-conscious-ness novel. The first phase she locates in the 1950s, the period when the socialist state was being forged, and she shows how prose narrative of this period tends to focus on positive heroines who serve as role models for the newly emerging society. The second phase takes place in the 1960s, and she links it to the campaigns for the improvement of women's education, showing how the heroines of this type of novel tend to be professional women rather than factory or agricultural workers, and how the novels emphasize the problems these women have in adapting to their new roles and in balancing the needs of society at large with their own personal needs. And while Anna Seghers is clearly the chief exponent of the *Aufbauroman*, so Christa Wolf emerges as the chief exponent of the *Ankunftsroman*. Her novel *Der Geteilte Himmel* ('The Divided Sky') published in 1963,[18] is not only about the two Germanies, but is also about the predicament of one woman, torn between the prospects of building a life for herself in a new socialist state and losing the man she loves. The third phase, according to Herminghouse, begins in the late 1960s, significantly the time when the women's movement as such begins to emerge in the West, and the emphasis shifts to writing about personal conflict and the crisis of identity. Had Patricia Herminghouse taken her analysis even further, she would have seen the problem of identity crisis emerge as the central theme of East German women writers in the 1970s and 1980s, expressed in a variety of ways, but most strikingly through the emergence of a new genre of Utopian fiction and a series of startling stylistic experiments.

In 1968, Christa Wolf wrote, in an essay entitled 'The reader and the writer':

The need to write in a new way follows a new way of living in the world, although there may be a time lag. 'One' hears, sees, smells, tastes in a different way at different times, at intervals that seem to get shorter. A change has occurred in one's perception of the world that even casts doubts on the unimpeachable memory; we see 'the world' once more – but what do we mean by the world? – in a different light; even feelings seem less permanent nowadays than in former times; there is a deal of confusion.[19]

This is an intensely personal statement but it has been quoted frequently and can be read as a statement about new East German literature and about writing by women whose life experiences are undergoing profound changes. Anna Seghers, during her lifetime, witnessed the rise and fall of Hitler, the creation of the GDR, the division of the city of Berlin, the horrors of bombing, starvation and rebuilding that drove women in their millions out of the homes to which they had been relegated under Nazism and into the streets armed with shovels and a will to survive. And in the latter years of her life she witnessed the emergence of women into public life at all levels, and the resulting demands made by women for the voice of their experiences to be heard alongside that of the men. It is therefore not so surprising to note that in 1970 her 'Strange Meetings'[20] tells about a girl living on earth who meets a man from another planet and another time. Two totally different visions and experiences encounter one another and the reader is confronted with a fundamental dualism.

The idea of duality, of division of the whole into two parts, recurs again and again in East German women's writing. At times it is the duality of the Nazi past and the socialist present, at other times it is the divided Germany, the two halves that do not make up a whole, and yet again it is the separateness of women's experience from that of men. The idea of duality is particularly present in Christa Wolf's work and comes to be an integral part of her writing process. In a short piece written in 1966, which she calls

'Interview with myself', she talks about the development of the idea for *Nachdenken über Christa T.* ('The Quest for Christa T.'), published in 1968.[21] Asking herself the question what is the 'subject matter' of her novel, she answers herself:

There was no 'subject matter' that I felt impelled to write about, there is no 'region of life' in it that I could call its milieu, no 'content', no 'plot' that I could describe in a few sentences.[22]

Shortly afterwards, she suggests that she might be writing 'a kind of posthumous biography' of Christa T., and shows how this may have been the initial idea but that the process of writing has led to other results:

Later on, I noticed that the object of my story was not at all, or did not remain so clearly herself, Christa T. I suddenly faced myself. I had not foreseen this. The relations between 'us' – Christa T. and the narrator 'I' – shifted of themselves into the centre; the differences in character and the points at which they touched, the tensions between 'us' and the way they dissolved or failed to dissolve.

The blurring of the dividing line between character and narrator, between writer and subject, is even more obvious in her *Kindheitsmuster* ('A Model Childhood') published in 1976, which tells the story of two journeys – the journey of the author, with her teenage daughter Lenka, her husband and her brother, back to the small town in which she grew up in the 1930s. It is the first time she has been back to the town, now in Poland, since she undertook the other journey, the flight from the advancing Red Army in 1945. The horrors of that first journey, westward, are contrasted with the second journey, eastward, in the 1970s when the starving refugees and burned-out cities have become part of a past that no longer has any meaning for Lenka, growing up in the post-Vietnam era. Two sets of questions are continually asked in this book, by mother and daughter, as the mother tries to understand who and what she was and how that person relates to the person she is now, and the daughter questions the value of what seem to her to be self-indulgent memories. The gap between the generations is painfully clear throughout and perhaps nowhere more so than at the point at which the author tries to reconcile her present knowledge of the concentration camps with her childhood ignorance of their existence just a few miles from where she lived and with her daughter's unawareness of precisely what the camps were:

This Eichmann, Lenka asked the other day, who is this man? You all fell silent. Then you asked to be shown her history book. Ninth class, she said sullenly going to look for it among her discarded schoolbooks in a box in the basement.

Almost one hundred pages dealt with the Fascist dictatorship in Germany. You checked and discovered that the name Adolf Eichmann was not mentioned. Heinrich Himmler occurred twice, once quoted as saying: 'Whether other nations live in prosperity or die of starvation concerns me only insofar as we may need them as slaves for our culture. Otherwise I'm not interested' . . .

On page 207 of Lenka's schoolbook is a map – 6″ × 4″ – of 'Fascist concentration camps throughout Europe during World War II'. The towns aren't marked on the map. The North Sea and the Baltic Sea are indicated, as are the main rivers: sixteen larger black dots mark the major concentration camps. Five of these are underlined, to indicate that they were extermination camps. The map is studded with small dots ('secondary camps') and small crosses ('ghettoes'). You can physically sense Lenka's understanding, her first, of what kind of landscape her mother spent her childhood in. From the geographical location of the extermination camps Chelmo, Treblinka, and maybe also Maidenek, one can assume that transports of human beings destined for these camps passed also through L. on the eastern railway. Trains destined for Auschwitz and Belsen probably used the southern route. Never did Nelly hear anyone around her mention any such transport, neither during nor after the war. No one in her family worked for the German railways in those days.

Lenka says so far as she knew, most students in her class – including herself – hadn't examined the map very thoroughly.[23]

The author's rediscovery of Nelly, herself as a child, becomes another kind of journey and is paralleled by Nelly's own journey through pain and physical hardship to another stage of development. The novel charts the inner journey alongside the actual journey to and from the village L., so that the narrative functions on several levels. The child Nelly and the mature woman are two halves of a whole, just as the mother and daughter are two halves of another whole, only this time irreconcilable. Significantly, Christa Wolf uses the pronouns 'you' and 'she' throughout, only shifting into an 'I' narrative in the final paragraphs of the novel. In an interview with Karen Macpherson she commented on this pronoun shift and explained that the use of 'she' and 'you' corresponded to the deep psychological division within the narrator herself. She suggested that this split was particularly felt by her generation and arose from a desire to find her own identity. 'I presume this also affects writers and generations in other countries: I can only talk about these things as they are in the places I know.'[24]

That the search for identity may be a recurring theme in a number of literatures is an interesting question, but what is significant is the prominence this search assumes in the present work of East German women writers. Although insisting that there is no women's movement as such, East German women writers are producing a literature that appears to exemplify the kind of writing demanded by feminist theoreticians such as Hélène Cixous ('Woman must write herself: must write about women and bring women to writing') or Xavière Gauthier: 'As long as women remain silent they will be outside the historical process. But if they begin to speak and write *as men do*, they will enter history subdued and alienated; it is a history that, logically speaking, their speech should disrupt.'[25]

The question of what constitutes women's writing has been one of the most fascinating pursued since the late 1960s. Cixous and Gauthier, together with a number of other French, Italian and West German women, are concerned with the fundamental problem of whether women's writing as such can exist at all. What they argue is that the history of Western thought has been based on the belief in the power of the word, and in literate societies the word is an instrument of power for men, who control the legal, educational, military and civil systems that are the word in action. Gauthier argues that the whole linear grammatical system of language that is at the heart of European culture is based on one fundamental signifier: the phallus. For her, then, the pen and the phallus are the same instrument, and she therefore questions what it means when women use the pen: 'We can marvel at the fact that women are alienated enough to be able to speak the language of man'.[26] Pursued to its limits, this view of writing sees the principal creative contribution of women in silence, in the texts that might have been written had there been a language in which to write them but have never actually been written at all.

But since women do write, have written and will go on writing, we can ask whether there is a type of text that avoids the linear, forward-thrusting shape of the traditional male form. Various critics have pointed out the connection that is often easy to overlook, that between women writers and what different cultures perceive as avant-garde texts. From Sappho, possibly the first clearly identifiable voice in European literature, through Hrosvitha, one of the earliest playwrights after the end of the Roman empire, to the pioneers of novel writing in the eighteenth century and the present *nouveaux romanciers*, woman have innovated and adapted what Cixous calls the language of men to new forms. And the present debate about women's writing emphasizes the importance of the fragmented form – the diary, the autobiography, the text that is neither clearly fiction nor clearly documentary, the fantasy, the Utopian novel – as a mirror of the more fragmented life experience of women, divided as they are between a variety of roles. The new women's writing is therefore not only writing about women, an exploration of women's unique experience, but is also another kind of writing altogether, one which demands and produces new forms. That these new forms should be appearing in such profusion in the GDR, without the framework of a women's movement as such and in a context in which socialist realism has played such a key role, is a most interesting phenomenon.

If a new women's writing can emerge without a feminist context, what are the implications? A possible explanation may lie in the patterns of social reorganization of the GDR. The material position of the average East German woman is undeniably better than that of the average woman in capitalist countries, and the women's movement in many countries is still struggling to achieve tiny gains in areas that East German women have ceased even to consider problematic. The difficulties arise with the simultaneous emphasis on women's right to work and on the special relationship between woman and the family. The result of this combination is to give women more collective responsibility within society than probably at any other time in the history of Western culture, and it is out of this specificity of experience that the impulse for a new kind of writing is emerging. Women in the GDR are writing differently because they are experiencing differently; in theory at least they have equal labour rights and equal power in the workplace, but at the same time they are held collectively responsible for the family, the microcosmic state structure.

The burden thus placed on East German women is massive. Able to compete openly in the labour market, they nevertheless carry the weight of the symbolic responsibility of the family within a society still structured on a patriarchal model. Socialism offers a rethinking of property and labour relations, but has not come up with a rethinking of sex relations; and so the paradox exists wherein women hold both practical and symbolic power and responsibility (a situation that one would associate with matriarchy) in a paternalistic, if not downright patriarchal, society. The absurdity of this inherently contradictory position provides the stimulus for the new women's writing. It is a mistake to read into the work of writers like Helga Königsdorf and Irmtraud Morgner any attack on the fundamental principles of socialism, but at the same time their works are full of savagely ironic comments on the untenable nature of women's position. Women have the possibility of juggling work and home life, but the strength required to keep the act together is massive. Some women, unwilling to face the strain of attempting so much, have begun to make certain choices – the birth rate has declined as more women refuse motherhood or opt for one child only, and many of those who do have children choose to stay longer at home. The irony of this situation is being brought out in the many novels and stories being written by women at the present: if the burden of work and family is intolerable, can the answer be merely a return to the kitchen sink on a full-time basis or a career at the expense of children? And underneath it all is the basic question: why in this new society have men not had to face a similar choice?

Discussing the new women's writing in the GDR, Irmtraud Morgner states: 'Anyone who lives in a different way on the social level must have a different way of writing.'[27] Engels points out that economic production and the production of people in the sex–gender sphere both determine the social organization of particular epochs and nations. What is happening now is therefore a predictable state in the development of a change in sex–gender roles. The problem remains of how men perceive those social changes, which they experience only at a second-hand level.

Perhaps the most striking feature of the new East German women's literature, however, is the passion in the writing.

To Western eyes, East German society appears well-ordered, the residue of stiff Prussian bureaucracy still apparent under different labels, and in this context women are appearing as the strongest and loudest radical voices around. With the practical problems lifted from women's shoulders to a greater extent than they have been for their sisters in the West, what is emerging in the GDR is a sense of powerful exuberant energy channelled through creativity, which finds an eager response from readers. It is interesting also to speculate about the market that the new women's literature is filling, the market that in Britain and America would be filled with romantic pulp novels, mainly about women raising their social status through a socially advantageous marriage. In the absence of a pulp-fiction market and the ideology behind it, East German women read the literature of women who question. Talking to the staff of *Für Dich*, the most widely read woman's magazine, which contains pieces of serious interest besides the usual cookery, knitting and fashion, I was told about the readership's demand for more fiction, for entertainment rather than instruction. The new women's literature fills precisely this gap.

In repudiating bourgeois feminism, East German women writers reject the concept of separatism, but nevertheless the depiction of men in novels and films made by women is often starkly critical. The young man who disrupts the lives of the women workers in Iris Gussner's film, *Alle Meine Mädchen*, ('All My Girls'), becomes the focal point of two separate but linked criticisms. On the one hand he is the intellectual, the film-maker who goes to live in the factory in order to use it for other purposes. He is therefore the bourgeois figure who enters in a higher status than the workers themselves. And then, of course, he is a man in an all-women context. Inevitably, he arouses sexual conflicts amongst the women, has an affair with one of them, stirs up feelings of sexual jealousy and disrupts the working relationship among them. Sex and class are inexorably linked in this film, and we are invited to look sympathetically at the women whose value system and sense of sisterhood is threatened by the male outsider. Significantly, this film was a great success in the GDR. Likewise, in Irmtraud Morgner's novel *Leben und Abenteuer der Trobadora Beatriz nach Zeugnissen ihrer Spielfrau Laura* ('Life and Adventures of Beatriz, Troubador, according to the Testimony of her Accompanist Laura'), men are portrayed unsympathetically right from the start. Beatriz is the twelfth-century wife of a Provençal count, who falls in love with a nobleman and composes verse to him. By this she offends on two levels: she reverses the convention that allowed a man to court another man's wife and decreed that the lady was always unattainable, and she writes directly and openly about her own feelings, defying literary convention. Since both are a sign of her utter madness, she comes to an arrangement with Persephone to allow her to sleep for eight hundred years and wake up in an age that will appreciate her better. She is woken by the curses of a man building a new motorway through the hedge of roses that surrounds her resting-place, and finds herself in 1968, in the France of student protests. From that moment onwards, she begins to explore her strange new world, making disconcerting discoveries about the hopes she has held for a new social order, but then meeting Laura and learning about the struggle for alternatives. In her summing-up of the life of Beatriz at the end of the book, Laura relates how she passed through a land where women worked as hard as men but were paid less, and ends on a Utopian note:

Then the inhabitants, in proletarian solidarity throughout the world, even overthrew the barrier of the family. And that of course was the garden of marvels, the promised land.[28]

The garden of marvels will come about when the final barrier, the family, is removed. In a state in which so much

84

emphasis is placed on the family and on the role of women within the family, the impact of that suggestion is keenly felt. Irmtraud Morgner satirizes the assumptions that men hold about women at the same time as she satirizes institutionalized practices that subordinate women, and the form she chooses, that of the modern fairy-tale, allows her the licence she needs. So successful was the saga of *Trobadora Beatriz* that she wrote a sequel, linked by the faithful *Spielfrau* Laura, *Amanda: ein Hexenroman* ('Amanda: a Witch Novel') that appeared in 1983.

Another writer who uses the fairy-tale or fantasy is Helga Königsdorf. In her collection of short stories *Meine Un-gehörigen Träume* ('My Outrageous Dreams'), published in 1978, one story in particular, 'Bolero', illustrates the new sense of feminist consciousness that speaks equally to women in East and West. The first-person narrator of 'Bolero' tells how one day she threw her unpleasant lover over a balcony almost casually and without any malice at all:

All the rest happened quite unexpectedly. We were eating in more of a rush than usual, because he hadn't let them know at home. Then he rushed out onto the balcony, already dressed but just in his stockinged feet and leaned over the balustrade to look at his car. While he was stretching over, on tiptoe, I got hold of his feet and lifted his legs up. He didn't even try to hang on, he was probably too taken aback. That would explain why it was so long before he screamed. He was already passing the seventh or sixth floor. I threw his shoes after him and his overcoat. I tidied the house, had a bath and sat down near the open door of the balcony. Ravel's *Bolero* filled the room in growing waves of sound.[29]

This kind of grotesque incident, so close to much of the feminist writing in capitalist countries, is by no means unusual. Increasingly, women writers are using the fairy-tale, the fantasy, the dream landscape for social critiques. By inventing new forms and playing so openly with existing ones, women writers in the GDR are perhaps closer to having created 'women's writing' than their sisters within the framework of organized women's movements and feminist consciousness.

A considerable part of this chapter has been spent in looking at women as creative artists, because it is on this level in particular that the changes in East German women's consciousness are most apparent. The problem of the unhappy marriage between Marxism and feminism is still very real for women in Western cultures. For women in the GDR and other socialist societies, that problem has to be viewed from a completely different perspective. They have to consider the implications of a newly defined set of social structures, in which traditional patterns of class consciousness have been unmade and replaced by something else. Academic women in the GDR may feel that they are well on the way towards an enlightened society in which the position of women has been radically redetermined, but for working-class women, out in the countryside or in the towerblocks of the new suburbs of Berlin, a lot of problems remain unsolved. The re-education of men is barely in its infancy.

In her recent book, *The Hearts of Men*,[30] Barbara Ehrenreich suggests that the US women's movement is directly linked to changes in the family structure that made men unwilling to support women and children financially as in previous generations. In other words, with the rising divorce rate, there was also a rise in the number of women below the poverty line; and the need for both financial and moral assistance led logically to a process of women organizing themselves to supply that help. If her thesis is valid, and it does go some way towards explaining the widespread support gained by the new Right and the Moral Majority, then it is difficult to see how any such development could take place in the GDR, where welfare services are freely available and where co-operative structures for living and working provide men and women with a range of support groups. Ehrenreich is suggesting that feminism is bound up with the way in which capitalist society reinforces male supremacy, a very different starting point from that of women in th GDR.

The persistence of Western writers in seeing the absence of a women's movement in socialist societies as evidence of the failure of *socialism* is therefore misleading. The West German collection of essays entitled *Wie Emanzipiert Sind die Frauen in der DDR?* ('How emancipated are women in the GDR?') is typical of this misconception. The original title of that collection of essays when published in Leipzig in 1978 was simply *Zur Gesellschaftlichen Stellung der Frau in der DDR* ('On the Social Status of Woman in the GDR'), and the subsequent title shows the change in reader expectations.[31] Starting with the assumption that a realignment of women's position in the labour market will lead to emancipation, both socialist and non-socialist theorists in the West assume that the expressions of discontent by East German women writers can be taken to signify the failure of the socialist system. In reality, the dialectics of the East German woman question are infinitely more complex than might appear at first glance.

There is little doubt that the situation for East German women with regard to daily social, labour and economic relations is an improvement on that experienced by women in most other societies, but equally there is little doubt about the voices raised in protest against the burdens placed on women's shoulders. Alongside the expressions of hope of a new beginning, such as those of philosopher Renate Feyl, are murmurings of complaint about the roles women are expected to play, balancing the traditional roles of mother, wife and companion with the newer ones of comrade, workmate and active member of the community. When they cleared away the rubble of the bombed cities women were intent on survival, but now that survival is more than assured they are beginning to demand more.

Discussing the problems a writer has to face in looking for a language with which to chart the processes of change, Christa Wolf argues:

We cling to the conventions, we consolidate the content of old ideas instead of seeking for new. We pacify instead of disturb and activate.[32]

Women writers in the GDR have started to disturb, looking for a way to articulate the changes in consciousness felt by more and more women for whom the process of daily fragmentation is hard to tolerate. And in a society as intensely literate as the GDR, the book is an instrument of considerable power, a way of reaching a wide audience. Moreover, in choosing to experiment with form, to produce fairy-tales, fantasies, multi-voiced novels, women writers express their anxieties in strikingly memorable ways. As Amanda, heroine of Irmtraud Morgner's witch novel, says: 'Art isn't truth. Art is a life that teaches us to understand truth.'[33]

Notes

1 For statistical information on the GDR see the publications brought out in English by Panorama DDR, Berlin, especially *Families in the GDR* (1983) and *Women and Socialism* (1983).
2 Interview with author.
3 B. Einhorn, 'Socialist emancipation: the women's movement in the German Democratic Republic', *Women's Studies International Quarterly,* vol. 4, no. 4 (1981) pp. 435–52.
4 J. Stephenson, *The Nazi Organization of Women* (London: Croom Helm, 1975), p. 18.
5 Stephenson, *Nazi Organization*, p. 145.
6 Stephenson, *Nazi Organization*, p. 13.
7 J. Quataert, 'Unequal partners in an uneasy alliance: women and the working class in imperial Germany' in M. Boxer and J. Quataert (eds) *Socialist Women: European Socialist Feminism in the 19th and Early 20th Century* (New York: Elsevier, 1978), pp. 112–45.

8 V. I. Lenin, *Women and Society* (from his speech at the November, 1918 First All-Russian Women's Congress) (New York: International Publishers, 1938) pp. 11–13.

9 In *Neue Deutsche Literatur*, no. 2 (1978), pp. 52–62.

10 M. Wander, *Guten Morgen, du Schöne* (Berlin: Aufbau-Verlag, 1977).

11 Here and elsewhere in the chapter, English quotations from articles or books published in German are my own translations.

12 M. Wander, *Tagebücher und Briefe* (Berlin: Aufbau-Verlag, 1981).

13 S. Kirsch, Die Pantherfrau: *Fünf Unfrisierte Erzählungen aus dem Kassettenrecorder* (Berlin and Weimar: Aufbau-Verlag, 1974).

14 E. Runge, *Frauen: Versuche zur Emanzipation* (Frankfurt am Main: Suhrkamp Verlag, 1970).

15 Wander, *Guten Morgen,* p. 78.

16 C. Wolf, *The Reader and the Writer* (Berlin: Seven Seas, 1977) p. 141.

17 P. Herminghouse, 'Wunschbild, Vorbild oder Porträt? Zur Darstellung der Frau im Roman der DDR', in P. U. Hohendahl and P. Herminghouse, *Literatur und Literaturtheorie in der DDR* (Frankfurt am Main: Suhrkamp Verlag, 1976), pp. 281–334.

18 C. Wolf, *Der Geteilte Himmel* (Berlin: Aufbau-Verlag, 1963).

19 Wolf, *Reader and Writer,* pp. 177–215.

20 A. Seghers, 'Sonderbare Begegnungen' (Strange meetings) in *Erzählungen 1963–1977* (Berlin: Aufbau-Verlag, 1977), pp. 415–529.

21 C. Wolf, *The Quest for Christa T.* (London: Hutchinson, 1971).

22 Wolf, *Reader and Writer,* pp. 76–83.

23 C. Wolf, *A Model Childhood* (New York: Farrar, Strauss & Giroux, 1980), pp. 235–6.

24 K. Macpherson, 'Interview with Christa Wolf', *GDR Monitor,* no. 1 (1979).

25 H. Cixous, 'La jeune née', and X. Gauthier, 'Existe-t-il une ecriture de femme?' in E. Marks and I. de Courtivron (eds and trans.), *New French Feminisms* (Brighton: Harvester, 1981), pp. 90–8, 161–4.

26 Marks and Courtivron, *New French Feminisms,* pp. 162.

27 *Frauenoffensive,* no 5 (1976), p. 39.

28 I. Morgner, *Leben und Abenteuer der Trobadora Beatriz nach Zeugnissen ihrer Spielfrau Laura* (Berlin: Aufbau-Verlag, 1974), p. 688.

29 H. Königsdorf, *Meine Ungehörigen Träume* (Berlin: Aufbau-Verlag, 1978), p. 15.

30 B. Ehrenreich, *The Hearts of Men: American Dreams and the Flight from Commitment* (New York: Doubleday, 1983).

31 H. Kuhrig and W. Speigner, *Wie Emanzipiert sind die Frauen in der DDR* (Cologne: Pahl Rugenstein, 1979), originally *Zur Gesellschaftlichen Stellung der Frau in der DDR* (Leipzig: Verlag für die Frau, 1978). Einhorn ('Socialist emancipation') has pointed out that far more East German feminist texts are republished in West Germany, and thus made available, than happens in reverse.

32 Wolf, *Reader and Writer*, p. 202.

33 I. Morgner, *Amanda: Ein Hexenroman* (Berlin: Aufbau-Verlag), p. 656.

Chapter Three

Italy

The most striking aspect of the development of feminist consciousness in Italy is the speed with which discussion of specifically women's issues gathered impetus in the 1970s. The two major focal points were, of course, the campaign to decriminalize abortion and the campaign to change the old fascist family law and introduce divorce. The growing numbers of women involved in protest marches on these issues testifies to an increased articulation of the needs of a hitherto silent majority. From the early beginnings of the movement, when small groups of women on the Left began to meet together to protest about being treated as 'angels of the copying machine' by their comrades in the student protests of the late 1960s – it was in 1968 that the ironic slogan 'Da angelo del focolare ad angelo del ciclostilo' ('From angel of the hearth to angel of the copying machine') was coined – the growth was so rapid that a pro-abortion protest march in December 1975 in Rome was attended by some 20,000 women, a number that had swollen to 50,000 on subsequent marches in April 1976 and June 1977.

Moreover, besides campaigns on issues which had traditionally been supported by parties on the Left, large-scale feminist protests against rape and criminal violence against women grew in frequency and in intensity. The trial of the men who raped and murdered Rosaria Lopez in a villa in

Circeo, near Rome, in 1976 proved the starting point for a massive demonstration against male violence, as did the trials of the rapists of Christina Simeoni in Verona in the same year and of Claudia Caputi in Rome in 1977. The first of the Riprendiamoci la Notte (Reclaim the Night) marches in Rome in 1976 was attended by some 10,000 women, and in March 1978 Italian women hosted an international conference on 'women and violence', an issue which looks like being a crucial one through the second half of the 1980s.

Even the most cursory glance at the history of Italian feminism shows a violence that distinguishes Italy from the rest of Europe, and if we consider the development of a women's movement in three separate stages it is possible to see a disturbing escalation of violence, both within the movement itself and against it from outside. And side by side with this escalation of violence there is a complex process of theorization, a thinking-out of basic assumptions concerning the role of women in social and political life in Italy, that sets Italian feminism apart as a highly articulate and intellectual phenomenon. In this sense, of course, it reflects the high level of political literacy in Italy. We should not forget, for example, the hundreds of thousands of people who came out of houses, factories and offices to demonstrate their solidarity with the murdered socialist President Allende of Chile in 1973, or the huge marches in support of the Portuguese revolution or, earlier, against American involvement in Vietnam. The poisoning of Seveso by a cloud of toxic gas in 1976 and the massacre at the Bologna railway station by a fascist bomb attack in 1980 led to millions joining mass rallies in the streets throughout the country. The continual crisis of governments in Italy, together with the large number of political parties and factions, a phenomenon often considered comic by Anglo-Saxons used to a two-party system, is testimony not so much to a lack of political awareness in the country as a whole but rather to an extremely sophisticated critical attitude to politicians and organizational structures in general. The proliferation of rallies, debates, *assemblee*, marches and mass demonstrations reveals a continuous active involvement in the processes of government by very large numbers of people from all classes of Italian society.

Broadly speaking, the three stages of the growth of Italian feminism can be linked to major events affecting the nation as a whole. The first period runs from the Risorgimento, through the spread of fascism, the Second World War and the anti-fascist resistance, to the civil war and the final emergence of Italy in 1945. The second period extends through the years of cold war, the growth of the Italian Communist Party (PCI) to its present position as the largest communist party in Europe outside the eastern block countries, and the period of student revolt in the late 1960s. The third period, in which Italian feminism is placed today, begins in 1977, the year of the 'historic compromise' between the PCI and the Christian Democrats which was widely perceived as a sell-out of basic socialist principles in the interests of acceding to government at any cost. Moreover, the outbreak of war between China and Vietnam raised for many Italian feminists the question of the viability of post-revolutionary societies still based on what was perceived as an essentially patriarchal vision. Manuela Fraire, leading theoretician and feminist, interviewed on the Italian radio station Radiotre in February 1979 stated her belief that all revolutions had been incomplete. In reply to a question asking whether the October Revolution, the Chinese revolution and the various anti-colonial movements of the twentieth century had all been illusory, she replied simply:

They are incomplete. They have only done half of what a revolution aims for. They didn't consider half the sky.

Growing dissatisfaction with what came increasingly to

be seen as male political life has led to an escalation of overt anti-male feeling. If we look at some of the most popular women's slogans of the 1970s the process of women's alienation from men, and, simultaneously, increased antagonism to men can be clearly seen. In 1970 the famous 'Donna è bello' slogan was coined, translated inadequately as 'woman is beautiful', but depending for effect on the use of the masculine ending for the adjective *bello* instead of the grammatically correct *bella*, thus raising the question of linguistic discrimination, an issue that has equally concerned women's groups in France and Germany.

Slogans during the massive abortion and divorce campaigns of 1972 – 5 were often direct and to the point:

Figli desiderati = figli amati	Wanted children = loved children
Divorzio subito	Divorce now
Diciamo no	Let's say no (i.e. to the referendum on divorce reform, deliberately and provocatively worded to ask Italians to say 'no' to preserving the status quo; a similar technique was employed in the British Common Market referendum)
Facciamoci sentire	Let's make ourselves heard
Non siamo organi da riproduzione. Donne lottiamo per l'emancipazione	We aren't just reproductive organs. Women, let's fight for our freedom
Non più puttane, non più madonne finalmente solo donne	Not whores any longer, not madonnas any longer, at last we can just be women

But already by 1976 another note was emerging in the slogans carried on the marches and used in women's rallies. Instead of the generalized statements demanding freedom or demands for specific rights, slogans often contained messages of hatred and warning to certain politicians in particular and to men in general.

Aborto si, me non finisce qui	Abortion yes, but it doesn't stop here
Non più madri, non più figlie, distruggiamo le famiglie	No longer mothers, no longer daughters, we're going to destroy families
Maschi, affogherete nella merda	Males, you'll drown in your own shit
Palle bianche, palle nere, vi tagliamo quelle vere	White balls, black balls, we'll cut off your real balls (this slogan relies on the pun of *palle* meaning also 'lies')
Oggi in piazza per abortire, domani in piazza col fucile	Today we're in the street to get abortions, tomorrow we'll be in the streets with guns.

At the demonstration protesting at the murder of Rosaria Lopez one slogan read:

Per Rosaria Lopez non basta il lutto, pagherete caro, pagherete tutto	Mourning's not enough for Rosaria Lopez, you'll pay dearly, you'll pay everything

And at a rally in 1977 another slogan attacked Enrico Berlinguer, head of the PCI:

La donna proletaria non si tocca, Enrico Berlinguer, ti spareremo in bocca	Don't touch working class women, Enrico Berlinguer, we'll shoot you in the mouth

Probably the most popular slogan of the 1970s, however, and the one which has lasted longest and been used repeatedly, is the famous

Tremate, tremate, le streghe sono tornate	Tremble, tremble the witches are back

Women dressed as witches, carrying broomsticks, marched

on the Reclaim the Night rallies chanting this slogan that has now become almost emblematic of Italian feminism.

The significance of witches in the Italian context pulls together a complex net of lines of discrimination against women. Firstly, and perhaps most obviously, is the notion of witches as outsiders, beyond the embrace of Mother Church, and, since the abortion and divorce campaigns drew on a reservoir of anti-ecclesiastical feeling, a good deal of the antagonism of women in the early 1970s was directed against the Vatican. Secondly, the use of the word *strega* as a term of abuse of women raises the question of linguistic discrimination and becomes part of the conscious attempt by women to reshape the language and re-evaluate terminology and categories. Thirdly, in affirming the new status of witches, Italian women affirm also their intention to re-structure history (and it is significant that women's movements through Europe and the United States have focused on the period of witch persecution as a way of shedding new light on the position of women in the shaping of modern society). Fourthly, the new *streghe* are drawing on the traditional idea of the power of witches and the fear inspired by the idea of that power. In short, by calling themselves *streghe* and identifying with the witches of the past, Italian women are working, as Mary Daly would put it, as 'Hag-ographers/Hag-ologists, uncovering our Prehistory, our Crone-ology'[1] and at the same time are seeking to establish a new power basis.

While the witch motif steadily acquired more prominence, so the anxiety caused by this new assertion led to other consequences. In the decade between 1970–1980 there was a growing number of reported cases of rape and violent assault on women throughout Italy. It is useless to speculate whether, as some would have us believe, the increase in statistics of rape in Western societies is directly attributable to men seeking revenge on a new generation of 'castrating women', nor does it serve much purpose to argue that perhaps it is not the incidence of rape that has increased but rather the incidence of rape being reported, due to a newly established sense of identity in women. The fact remains that rape cases are given prominence in the media, and both men and women have come to believe that rape is one of the fastest-growing crimes in Western society. In Italy, where even in the 1960s the rape of a village girl was often set up as a means to force the victim to marry her attacker against her will, there have been a series of cases of gang rape and murder that have shocked the nation and united women's groups in protest against male violence as a whole.

Alongside the number of documented cases of rape are details of other incidents of violent aggression against women. At a demonstration in Rome in 1977 Giorgiana Masi died as a result of police brutality, while at party rallies women have detailed cases of attacks against them by their own male comrades. In February 1977, for example, during an occupation at the University of Rome, women students closed their assemblies to male colleagues as a result of attacks against them, and similar measures were taken at the University of Padua in the same year. In January 1979, in one of the most serious incidents of all, neo-fascist gunmen broke into the recording studios of Radio Donna, the independent all-women radio station in Rome, shooting and seriously wounding several women.

The cases of violence against women, which are used by one school of feminist theoreticians to show the total impoverishment of male social organization, are countered by another school of thought that matches violence with violence of a similar kind. The involvement of women in the Red Brigade, or the female terrorist squads such as the commando groups that shoot key figures of the male establishment in the knees, are examples of a different kind of feminism, one which seeks to set up a new power structure for women based not on idealized terms but on the same terms as those claimed by men as a basis for revolution. Such feminists face a very crucial problem: if women define themselves through their alienation, through what they do not have, what they are excluded from, if they perceive themselves as reduced to a commodity, how can they become the active role-players in a revolutionary context? In choosing to play an active part, therefore, the new Italian women terrorist squads see themselves as an affirmative rather than as a negative revolutionary force, defining themselves not by what they do not have but by what they feel they are entitled to possess.

Ironically, although the phenomenon of female terrorism is perceived by the majority of Italian feminists as emulative of men and undesirable, there is a way in which such activities can be seen as the mainstream of Italian feminist development. For the role played by women in the unification of Italy and in the resistance to fascism was essentially one of active military participation. Garibaldi as the man of action of the Risorgimento is matched by Anita Garibaldi, whose participation in the Redshirt campaigns assured her of a place in Italian folklore equivalent to that of Britomart, Ariosto's fighting heroine. Moreover, with the acceleration of industrial growth that followed unification in 1870, the whole issue of women as a large-scale labour force began to emerge, together with the related issue of professional training for women. Active feminists such as Anna Kulisci-off, Anna Maria Mozzoni and Emilia Maraini, starting from different political positions, drew attention to the paradox of an increased female labour force unmatched by an increase in women actually making decisions about the deployment of that labour. Women, they argued, were being used to create the new Italy but were being given no say in determining what the new Italy ought to be. A series of strikes by women workers in the late 1870s and again throughout the 1890s were put down with considerable violence. In 1898, for example, following a demonstration against the rising cost of bread, some thirty-six women were arrested in Milan alone, one of whom was Anna Kuliscioff.

By 1910 the 'National Committee for Women's Suffrage' had been set up and two years later militant women socialists in Milan established a journal entitled *La difesa della lavoratrice* ('The Defence of the Working Woman'). At the same time, together with agitation by women workers for better pay, better working conditions, parity of treatment and a share in the decision-making processes, another major focus of feminist protest was the lack of educational facilities for women. Anna Maria Mozzoni attempted to elaborate a scheme for an alternative education for women, in which one component was to have been the study of the conditions and history of women in different nations, but her plan never got off the ground. In her useful book, Maria Rosa Cutrufelli quotes a letter from the headmistress of a Rome technical school, written as late as 1900, which gives an insight into the prevailing attitudes conditioning the education of women:

Physical deterioration of our race will certainly occur if the education of females is over-emphasized, because the realm of the household will no longer seem to smile at a woman, she will be drawn to the lures of the struggle for existence . . .
Alternating study with domestic chores strengthens the mind, reinforces beliefs, makes the soul more serene, for our intellects cannot cope with continual tension and become dull and tired if thus abused.[2]

In 1906 two girls sat the exam for the *ginnasio* (grammar school), which had previously been reserved for boys only, and the process of opening higher levels of education to women began to accelerate. Earlier, in 1878 De Sanctis had opened two institutes of higher education to women wanting to train as teachers in primary schools. The notion that at best women might be able to teach very young children, an extension of the mothering role, seems to have been strongly held and was to surface again in the fascist period, when a policy of returning women to the bosom of the family from professional arenas was institutionalized and legalized.

During the First World War the woman question took on an extra dimension, as women workers were employed on a vast scale in the factories of northern Italy. Camilla Ravera, the grand old lady of the Italian women's resistance, has described how women workers were the initiators of the great strike in Turin in 1917 against the duration of the war and the food shortages. She has also described how groups of women, although not party members, continued to attend meetings organized by the PCI in the early 1920s and how, in Milan and Turin, these groups were often organized into district committees to discuss localized problems that mainly conerned women. At such meetings women took an active part, even organizing crèches for small children.

With the growth of fascism, such groups were eliminated and the dominant ideology relegated women to the idealized role of mothers and companions of the new heroes. In the seventh of her series of interviews on Radiotre on the general topic of women and politics, Rossanna Rossanda, former communist partisan, attempted to explain why women were attracted to fascism even though in both theory and practice it relegated women to secondary status. For example, successive edicts on education barred women from studying certain subjects in the schools, denied them the right to become headmistresses of schools above the primary level, even doubled the fees of women students in the universities. Yet, in an interview with Luisa Brolis, a woman who later became a partisan but only after some years of total commitment to fascism, one crucial detail of Brolis's early faith in the fascist order was brought to light: the notion that fascism was a means of restoring pride in a nation bruised after the long years of war and suffering and the acute food shortage, and a means of restoring order, of ending street violence and worker's protests. The violence, Luisa Brolis recalled, was reported in the newspapers as originating not with the fascist brigades but with the brutality of workers who, by their impossible demands on the state at a time of economic crisis, were merely demonstrating their lack or patriotism, their 'bolshevism'. In other words, the selling of fascism as a liberating force was so effective that many women failed completely to perceive the extent of their own oppression and were taken in by the superficial exaltation of women as 'protagonists' in a new scenario. For, in Mussolini's version, Anita Garibaldi did not so much fight hand to hand together with her man in the cause of creating a new classless society, she stood alongside him as his mainstay and support, creating the home and family towards which the vision of a new world was directed.

The apparent collaboration of Italian women with fascism is still a central and thorny problem with which feminists are attempting to deal. Maria Antonietta Macciocchi, for example, considers the problem from the viewpoint of the psychosexual determinants of mass politics and sees Mussolini as a kind of mystic husband, an animus figure to whom women gave their gold wedding-rings in hundreds of thousands on 18 December 1935, the famous Day of Wedding Rings, receiving little iron bands from il Duce in return. Macciocchi takes up Brecht's comparison of the relationship between women and fascism to that of whores and their pimps and widens the discussion by relating fascism to religion:

In a political regime the question of the influential and active support of women is connected with the superstructure of its most dense form, namely religion. It is at the very moment when religion, the centuries-old scourge of women, is no longer adequate as an ideological shield for the power apparatus of the rising bourgeoisie (the entry of female power as a force in the struggle occurred in the nineteenth and twentieth centuries with the Paris Commune and the October revolution) that fascism comes to the relief of the church guards. It is able to do this because of the submissiveness of women, whose instincts it can channel into a sort of new religious fervour which serves to support mass dictatorships and mass totalitarian regimes. The seizure of power by fascism and nazism uses as levers the martyred, baneful and necrophiliac femininity of the widows and mothers of men killed in the first world war, and the femininity of Woman as Reproducer of the Species (which is associated with female madness). This raises an issue which goes to the heart of the actual power struggle, whatever it may be. Adolf Hitler affirmed that 'in politics, it is necessary to have the support of women, because the men will follow spontaneously.'[3]

Although Macciocchi seems to disregard developments in Italian feminism in the nineteenth century (due to her particular methodological approach which focuses on the history of fascism only), the issues that she raises are fascinating and provocative. The relationship between the Mazzinians, for example, and the Vatican is vastly different from the relationship between church and the state in the early 1900s, and one of Mussolini's major steps towards a reaffirmation of that second-stage relationship was the Lateran Pact of 1929, which again gave the church a powerful say in the private life of the individual Italian and enshrined the concept of the indissoluble family in state as well as canon law. Pope Leo XIII had asserted in 1880 that 'the man rules the woman as Christ rules His Church', and in view of the low level of education for women, especially in the impoverished south, it is perhaps not so surprising that women embraced fascist ideology, because they genuinely perceived Mussolini's propaganda as placing them in a position of higher esteem by preserving the status quo. The problem currently being tackled by feminists across the world – the paradox of defining a woman by what she *is* rather than by what she *does* – can be seen at its clearest in a period of economic entrenchment such as the one in which Mussolini and Hitler rose to power. The denial of active participation in what the pre-fascist Roman headmistress described as 'the struggle for existence' can be offset by an assertion of the intrinsic values of 'being' – hence women could be gradually eliminated from teaching and studying in institutes of higher education but rewarded with medals for producing children. In this way it is possible to kill two birds with one stone: to reinforce the ideology set out by Pope Leo *and* to reinforce class barriers amongst women, since the educated middle-class woman and the militant female worker are isolated from the female majority who remain in the home as housewives and mothers. The same process can be discerned time and again in twentieth-century societies; Macciocchi cites post-Allende Chile as an example, and postwar Britain, with the spread of Bowlby's theories of maternal deprivation, can be seen as a manifestation of the same ideology at work.[4]

The extent of the commitment of Italian women to fascism is still a grey area, likely to be the subject of debates for a long time to come. Equally, the alternative history, of women in the resistance movement, is also vague and inadequately defined. Studies of the history of women's resistance tend to consist of personal accounts in which precise details of time, place etc. are not given. In a Radiotre interview, Lidia Menapace, a communist, discussed the problem of writing such a history and made some useful observations:

Who are 'the women of the Resistance'? Me, my generation, the women who had a foothold in politics, the known partisans, are we all really representative of what Italian women in the Resistance were like? Today various historians are writing books and collecting accounts of what they call the '*silent Resistance*', about the women who were on the sidelines, behind and beside the male partisans. How many of these were there? Impossible to say. But they were the ones who enabled the struggle of the partisans to happen and to survive. This help was *silent*, not in the sense that it might not have happened, but because often these women never wanted their names or identity to be recorded . . . But more generally, if I look at things from our point of view, what interests me is, if taking part in great events means direct political involvement, whether the overall political presence of women in the Resistance gives them a *decisive* role even though it was *silent*. In short, that there is normally a part of politics that is always silent and critical.[5]

Taking up this same point in a later broadcast, Rossanna Rossanda speculated on the numbers of women involved. Approximately 43,000 women are claimed to have fought with the resistance, and one set of official figures suggests that there were some 35,000 fighting partisans, 20,000 *patriote* and maybe about 70,000 enrolled in the *gruppi di difesa della donna*. Quoting a former partisan group leader who claimed that for every combatant in a guerrilla war there was a back-up of at least fifteen others who provided some kind of necessary assistance, almost all of whom were normally women, Rossanna Rossanda suggested that this would imply that some 2,000,000 women were actively involved in one way or another in the resistance and that official figures were hopelessly inadequate.

Camilla Ravera is in no doubt about the large number of women actively involved in the resistance, and she sees the part played by women as marking a high point in the history of both the struggle of Italian workers against fascism and the struggle of Italian women to achieve a greater measure of emancipation. She also sees the granting of the vote to women on 15 February 1945 as a direct result of the role of women in the resistance:

When the moment of the war of liberation arrived, it seemed like a miracle to everybody that the first groups of women partisans mobilized so quickly (they were our comrades who had come out of the secret organizations and taken on another role, arming themselves) and also it was an amazing phenomenon to see how the women got involved. There were hundreds and hundreds of women who enrolled in the ranks of the partisans as fighters. But there were thousands and thousands of women active in the Liberation Movement: they stored arms, carried arms, relayed orders, looked after the wounded, kept lines of communication open and so on. Not only that, but we met with solidarity and help in the most incredible situations. Always, whenever we were looking for shelter, some woman would help us. That underground work we had kept up during the fascist period gave undreamed-of results. The participation of women in the movement to liberate Italy from fascism and build a more just society actually signified their place in a new condition. Not for nothing was one of the first depositions among the laws established after Liberation the granting of the vote to women. And in the first Parliament of the Republic there were more than fifty women representatives. At that point in time women gave such a convincing, clear display of the fact that they did know how to think politically, how to choose, take decisions, get together even in struggle . . . And during the reconstruction, when there was still a sense of anti-fascist unity, women worked miracles.[6]

When we look at the apparent collaboration of large numbers of women with the dominant fascist ideology, and at the role of women in the resistance, it is possible to see a number of contradictions that are still causing problems for contemporary Italian feminists. The first, most obviously, concerns the place of women in the history of the period. If the active, military story of the women's brigades amongst the partisans is stressed, then it is possible to see how contemporary bands of armed women operating as urban guerrillas can conceive of themselves as part of a tradition. If, on the other hand, one considers what the struggles of the partisans actually achieved for women once the euphoria of the immediate victories wore off, then it is possible to see how a growing sense of dissatisfaction with the supposedly 'feminist' parties of the Left leads to an affirmation of female terrorism. Even Camilla Ravera admits that after the liberation and the granting of the vote to women there was a long period of stasis. She defends this to some extent by arguing that the most immediate task in hand was to organize the workers in the defence of their rights and to establish a mass basis for the proletarian movement to combat the possibility of any fascist counter-revolution. 'You have to remember', she maintains, 'that as a minority party we could have been overwhelmed. We had to turn ourselves into a mass party, but this involved total dedication to the day to day struggles for work and salaries that were absolutely essential.'[7] Faced with such problems, Camilla Ravera argues, the Communist Party and other parties of the Left chose to put the question of women to one side. The history of women in the resistance was merged in the history of the Italian people in the resistance.

In spite of the apparent failure, after 1945, to build a women's movement and to deal with the issues of abortion, reform of the old fascist family laws, etc., women on the Left were encouraged by the position of Palmiro Togliatti. In 1945 Togliatti declared that the woman question was not an issue that concerned only one party or class, and stressed the inevitable close link between the development of democracy and the emancipation of women. Teresa Noce, an early socialist (known in the 1920s as 'Terrore bianco' (the 'White Terror'), because she jokingly claims, she used so much face powder), feels that the PCI tried to see the woman question as part of wider issues, but blames herself and her female comrades for not having insisted on more sooner. Woman in the party, she claims, had not developed at the same pace as the party itself, in spite of their involvement in resistance to fascism. The needs of the party had begun to diverge from the needs of women in the new society in postwar Italy. Another old PCI member, Giorgina Levi, notes how a process of tacit discrimination applied in the party and continued for the next thirty years:

After the Resistance there was no discrimination, but women comrades were not pushed or helped or invited to take up higher positions. Women comrades didn't try to get into the important jobs, nor did men comrades think that a woman should . . . A woman as party branch secretary was inconceivable, whereas nowadays it's an established fact. Even Camilla Ravera, with all the years she spent in prison and the role of organization she carried out, was never secretary of the Turin branch. And yet still, compared with the other parties, the PCI was by far the most advanced. There was no concept of high-level women's politics, only a sort of middle level.[8]

It is therefore possible to see how the seeds of discontent with the treatment of women by the parties of the Left were already being sown even in the period of apparent success. Moreover, if later generations came to feel that the active participation of women in the resistance movement had failed to achieve much, does such an attitude imply that the women partisans had simply behaved as honorary men? And if the militarism of the women partisans were to be seen in such light, the heroines of the resistance would indeed be the 'silent fighters', the reserve of women who offered help to the anti-fascists. This would certainly seem to be the position of Lidia Menapace, who draws parallels between these women and the silent armies of the proletariat whose names have vanished, unrecorded in time.

The problem with such a concept returns us to one of the fundamental questions troubling contemporary Italian feminist thought: if there is an essentially female politics that the traditional historical forms of political thought and action have been unable to conceive, does such a politics reside in silence, in the space that women occupy, as it were, within the male-dominated social structures? The dangers of this concept are very apparent, for if one conceives of a female politics that exists apart from and within (male) politics as we know it, the line between the silent collaboration of women with fascism and the silent collaboration of women with the partisans is difficult to draw. Rossanna Rosssanda feels that the newly formed Italian women's movement has undergone two paradoxical processes. The first, she suggests, is the way in which the movement gathered momentum on central issues such as abortion and divorce-law reform, fighting those campaigns with allies from other movements, and then, once the unity provided by those causes ceased, began to become more isolated. The second is the way in which, in that isolation, the women's movement has turned in on itself, trying to analyse its own growth problems, and as a result has begun to split into fragmented units. Behind these processes, of course, are the questions whether women can and should conceive of a revolution on the same terms as men, whether any of the existing concepts of revolution can be applied, whether, indeed, the term has any meaning at all for women.

A major, if not *the* major issue of Italian feminist thought, which is thrown into sharp relief when we consider what I have termed the first period of Italian feminism up to 1945, is the question of determining whether such a thing as a separate women's discourse can exist. All the analysing and reanalysing of the role played by women in sustaining fascism, in opposing it and in building a post-fascist society after the war, returns us to the basic theoretical questions of the meaning of political participation and of the relationship of women to traditional concepts of power on the Right and on the Left.

One of the most significant documents of the Italian women's movement is the pamphlet *Sputiamo su Hegel* ('We spit on Hegel'), the manifesto of 'Rivolta Femminile, a separatist group that emerged in Rome and Milan in 1970, opposed to all forms of organization and hierarchy. Rivolta Femminile saw itself as distinct from all existing political parties and factions and constituted itself as encounter groups which eventually developed into the collectives of Lotta Femminile. Significant statements from the manifesto show that Rivolta Femminile perceives issues as global:

Woman cannot be defined in relation to man. Both our struggle and our freedom are based on this assumption . . .

Woman is the Other with respect to man. Man is the Other with respect to woman.

Equality is an ideological attempt to enslave women on even higher levels.

To identify woman with man is to nullify our last road to freedom. Freedom, for women, does not mean accepting the same life as men because that is unlivable, it means expressing our own sense of existence . . .

The image of women through which man has perceived woman is his own invention . . .

We recognize marriage as the institution that has subordinated woman to man's destiny. We are opposed to marriage . . .

Women are fed up with educating sons that turn into bad lovers . . .

Behind every ideology we perceive a hierarchy of the sexes . . .

Feminism was the first political moment of historical criticism of the family and of society . . .

We have looked on for 4,000 years: now we have seen!

Behind us is the apotheosis of thousands of years of male supremacy. Institutionalized religions have been its strongest base. And the concept of the 'genius' has been set up as the unreachable high point . . .

Civilization has called us inferior, the church has called us sex, psychoanalysis has betrayed us, Marxism has sold us out to a hypothetical revolution.

We cite as evidence thousands of years of philosophical thought that has expounded the theory of woman's inferiority.

We hold the organizers of systems of thought responsible for the great humiliation the patriarchal world has exposed us to, for they have upheld the principle of woman as an additional being for the reproduction of mankind as a link with godliness or the threshold of the animal world; a private sphere and a *pietas.*

With metaphysics they have justified everything that was unjust and despicable in women's life.

We spit on Hegel.

Class consciousness as a revolutionary theory that developed out of the master-servant dialectic excludes woman just as badly.

We are reopening the discussion of socialism and the dictatorship of the proletariat . . .

Man's strength lies in identifying with culture, ours lies in denying it . . .

We are seeking an authentic gesture of revolt and we will not betray it either to organization or to proselytizing.[9]

The *Sputiamo su Hegel* manifesto, although clumsily expressed, can now be seen as very much ahead of its time, for Rivolta Femminile was concerned primarily with a woman's alternative to the male power bases and structures. By describing feminism as 'the first political moment of historical criticism of the family and of society', the manifesto is seeking to use the term 'political' in a new way. And by rejecting all forms of organization the manifesto dissociates itself from all parties or groups, feminist or not, that utilize what are perceived as inherently oppressive systems.

The anti-organizational premise of Rivolta Femminile and the later Lotta Femminile stands in direct contrast to the vision of the feminists of the traditional and new Left. This has led to a number of clashes over the years, as feminist unity over the major campaigns has begun to show signs of strain. Anti-feminists have pointed to the apparent fragmentation of what seemed in 1974–5 to be a united movement of angry women demanding immediate changes in the social order as evidence of failure, but this is clearly wrong. The gap between the feminist groups of the new Left and the more radical feminist groups in Italy is wide but not unbridgeable, for both sides are in search of a specifically feminist discourse. At the Modena Women's Conference in March 1979 the divisions were very marked, but behind the apparent clash of methods there could be discerned a common desire to explore the issues of women's creativity. At Modena, the anti-organizational feminists attacked the organizers of the conference structure itself, arguing that group discussion leaders, programmes of events and structured debates were inherently oppressive to women. The counter-argument maintained that, without minimal organization, women would sit in silence together for hours and achieve nothing. Silence, it was argued, was traditionally an instrument of oppression that men had imposed on women, and for women to impose it on themselves was worse than useless. The radical feminists held that organizational structures were élitist, the left-wing feminists countered that a lack of organizational structures would result in anarchy and the dissolution of unity. The conference split with bitter exchanges on both sides.

Behind the conflict the same problem can be seen again: how to determine a method and a language in which women can both define themselves and help themselves. And unlike the Anglo-Saxon feminists, who have laid such emphasis on self-definition through awareness of sexuality, or French feminists, who have utilized the instruments of psychoanalysis and theories of the unconscious, Italian feminists, even where seemingly most incompatible, are preoccupied with the same question that once preoccupied Machiavelli: the nature of power.

The writer Gianna Pomata suggests that the women's movement is linked to a series of bourgeois revolts against absolutism, and sets the development of feminism in a historical context, tracing what she calls the 'progressive' or 'evolving' history of women in Europe from the eighteenth century onwards.[10] Her theory of women's history as distinct from any other kind is based on the assumption that the idea of *woman* is an artificial male construct. Rather than considering the history of this construct, which seeks to explain the subordination of women in biological terms (the old 'why have there never been any women geniuses?' fallacy), she argues that women as individuals, repressed to greater or lesser degrees by the dominant system, have indeed left their mark, which can be clearly seen if looked at from a different perspective. The basis of her argument is the split between public and private, a patriarchal distinction that undervalues the private at the expense of the public and consequently diminishes the contributions made in anything except the public domain. A useful way of perceiving Gianna Pomata's argument is to consider the map of the world as a metaphor: a two-dimensional map which delineates national boundaries will yield a very different impression from that of a three-dimensional contour map showing the shape of mountain ranges, valleys, rivers etc. with no regard to national boundaries at all. If we compare the accepted notion of history (male-determined) to the two-dimensional national map, and the alternative notion to the three-dimensional contour map, it becomes possible to see how incredibly different perceptions can be according to how the basic material is ordered.

Gianna Pomata points out that an internationally accepted feminist slogan is the statement 'the personal is political' and observes that

For feminism, there is resemblance rather than opposition, and a connection between that which appears in private as residual authoritarianism left over from patriarchal power and that which is affirmed in the public sphere as growing rationality.[11]

The problem of redefining the meaning of power in feminist terms led to some distinctive and contradictory lines of thought in the 1960s and 1970s. Although it is possible to relate the emergence of a new phase of feminist consciousness to the widespread student unrest of the late 1960s, it is clear from the early statements of Italian feminist collectives that they perceived the woman question as a distinct area of struggle in its own right. In a pamphlet circulated at the University of Rome in 1969 by a group of women actively involved in the worker–student protests there is a statement which declares that the focus of attack must be capitalistic division of labour, and then goes on to spell out what this means for women. The struggle, claims the manifesto, must be against unpaid labour within the four walls of the home that only has an exchange value inside the family structure, and against the use of the family as a means of keeping an unpaid reserve force of workers for potential exploitation. In a rather confused and garbled manner, the manifesto continues on these lines, suggesting that the economic stability of the family structure reinforces the dominant ideology, and arrives at the conclusion that, in order that the capitalist division of labour may be attacked, the notion of the family as the ideological base of capitalist stability must first be destroyed.

But the most significant passage in the whole manifesto is an attack on male left-wing colleagues:

It is our own comrades in the struggle who don't understand the way in which women have been pushed to the sidelines in terms of their contribution to history and to production. They don't see the trap of underdevelopment in which women are caught nor the way in which this helps the capitalist system, they don't recognize *the economic and ideological ghetto that they are helping to perpetuate*, that turns women into the natural allies of the lower working class and blacks . . .

Already then, at this early stage, the sense of dissatisfaction with the policy of parties on the Left towards women can be discerned. The main reasons that this dissatisfaction did not fully realize itself until a few years later are undoubtedly the long-standing traditional links between left-wing politics and radical intellectual life and the split between older women seeking to base their feminism on European Marxist foundations and the younger generation attracted by the Maoist concepts of cultural revolution.

The stress on the family as the centre of ideological oppression, a theory that derives directly from Engels, was reinforced in the early 1970s by the major campaigns for the legalization of abortion and divorce. A pamphlet published by the Movimento di Liberazione della Donna (Women's Liberation Movement) in 1970 states bluntly:

In reality being a woman in Italy means living illegally, it means sooner or later becoming a criminal. Because it is an offence to use the pill – and an offence to have an abortion. And since women take the pill and have abortions in their millions, let anyone who is without sin throw the first stone.

Together with these rallying campaigns was the development of another, smaller offshoot of discontent with the family structure – the Wages for Housework campaign, which proposed salaries for women working in the home in order to reconstruct the basis of household labour relations. Similar campaigns, always on a small scale, emerged more or less simultaneously in several countries, but it seems clear that the theoretical basis of the Italian campaign was less divergent from the feminist mainstream than elsewhere. In Britain, for example, the Wages for Housework campaign attracted the attention of right-wing figures who perceived that payment to women for housework could be reconciled with the idealized image of woman as homemaker. But in Italy, where the image of the ideal family could so easily be perceived as a construct utilized by the church and various male politicians alike, the Wages for Housework campaign had more radical implications. It is interesting also to note that in the great mass of Italian published material attacking the nuclear family as anti-women, relatively little space is given to the question that British and American feminists have considered so extensively, i.e. the setting up of alternative structures based on concepts of power-sharing and the division of child care between mothers and fathers. Indeed, a marked feature of Italian feminist discussion is the absence of much discussion of child care at all. The campaigns for crèche facilities that have preoccupied women in Britain, for example, and the discussions of the nature of 'mothering' which feature in North American women's groups do not seem to have been of similar concern to Italian women. Instead, the emphasis is placed on the theoretical implications of family structures, and is allied to the discussion of what being a woman actually means.

An article appearing in *Quarto mondo, no. I* in March 1971, entitled 'La crisi della famiglia' ('The family in crisis') began by quoting Engels's famous statement on 'domestic slavery' and went on to argue that the concept of the conjugal family or 'nuclear' family is an unnatural structure, as much a product of history as any other type of family existing at any other time:

Authority and male supremacy are still the models on which the contemporary nuclear family is based, with the difference being that authoritarianism and the hierarchical principle were functional components of the productive economic activity of the pre-industrial patriarchal family. Nowadays the nuclear family has no productive function and is not even a unit providing its members with a sense of solidarity and mutual assistance (in spite of what we are told by priests, sociologists and politicians . . .)

This kind of family must be demolished. And it must be we women, as the most oppressed and most directly exploited members, who take on the task.

The notion of attacking the construct of the family and hence of challenging the idea of the family as a power base for a patriarchal social structure runs through most of the feminist writing of the 1970s, and it is easy to see why this should have become such a prominent feature of the women's movement in Italy. A rejection of the family implies a rejection of the particular image of woman as the madonna, bolstered for so long by the church, and given a new lease of life by fascism. Not for nothing is the classic insult a reference to the sexual activities of a man's mother or sister, in marked contrast to Anglo-Saxon insults that so often refer to female genitalia. The great body of Italian literature and painting returns again and again to the image of woman as both pure and maternal, the lover's ideal vision who descends to earth and reigns in glory in the kitchen.

In the 1960s, the period of economic boom in Italy, when

a new mass-consumer market opened up, heavy advertising propaganda was directed at women. However, in the marketing of the 'new life' through advanced technology (it is interesting to note that although English has to use a clumsy format for 'electrical appliance', Italian coined a new word *elettrodomestico*, an indication of the extent of the reorganization of the running of the home), care was taken to stress the continuation of the old values. Electrical appliances and tinned foods need not imply the destruction of the family, since they were not being sold as aids to busy working women but rather as status symbols of family advancement. And since the economic boom coincided with massive building programmes and with waves of immigration into urban centres from southern Italy and from the poorer mountain areas, the drive to acquire symbols of the new life became even stronger. By 1968 a family that had 'arrived' might be in the process of buying (as opposed to the earlier predominant system of renting property) a three-bedroomed luxury flat in a condominium in the suburbs, with shared use of a swimming-pool, electronically operated gates, tiled floors to replace the old-style marble and fully fitted kitchens in gleaming plastic complete with a full set of *elettrodomestici*, furnished with designer furniture mass-produced in the factories of Lombardy. Yet still the basic structure, with father as provider and mother dependent on father to keep up the mortgage payments, remained unchanged. Indeed, it is fascinating to discover that during the 1960s, the period of such expansion, the Italian women's workforce dropped by about a million. Part of this can be explained by a decline in the number of women employed in agriculture, but it is still a puzzling statistic. Adriana Seroni points out, however, that there was an increase in non-unionized part-time work for women, suggesting that the decline of women in full-time paid employment led to greater exploitation. Writing in July 1973, in the magazine *Donne e politica*, she succinctly sets out the contradiction between woman's position as receiver of the material products of the new economic boom and her plight outside the home:

Enormous riches belonging to the nation, basic requirements of civilisation, social products indispensable to the 'quality of life' have all been sacrificed on the altar of chaotic development of twisted private consumerism. In the wake of all this, woman, her image and her beauty have been degraded to serve a political vision that is both misguided, and, as we can clearly see today, failing. She has been shut out for the most part from production, and has been exalted as a symbol and an instrument of twisted consumerism. She has been denied crèches, nursery schools, full-time school for her children, any kind of tranquility in her motherhood, but at the same time her image – as mother too – has been used to advertise a certain brand of talcum powder or a special outfit, or some perfectly useless object presented as absolutely indispensable.

Besides being seen as a potential market for household goods and clothes, Italian women have been offered an astounding range of magazines and love-story journals, including the ubiquitous *fotoromanzo* (a love story in photographs set out in comic format, and introduced into Britain in teenage magazines in the late 1960s). In a book entitled *Perchè la stampa femminile?* ('Why Women's Publishing?'), a collection of essays and papers from the conference of the same title organized by the Ferrara Unione Donne Italiane in November 1976, Bruna Bignozzi, a teacher, points out that the first *fotoromanzo* appeared in 1947. By 1972 there were some sixty types of *fotoromanzo*, with titles such as *Charme*, *Darling*, *Sogno* ('Dream'), *Noi due* ('We Two'), *Idilio* etc. Analysing a variety of *fotoromanzi*, she notes the conservatism of the material and the way in which certain stereotyped images are reinforced: when a woman asserts herself by taking a degree, or trying to get a job, or travelling alone, she inevitably comes to grief, because she contravenes the norm of the woman whose ambition is to be happily married to a good man ('good' referring to appearance and social status). Bruna Bignozzi points out that the hero is almost always a member of the middle classes or the aristocracy, never a peasant or a mechanic. I myself have been struck by the recurrence in *fotoromanzi* of the late 1970s and early 1980s, after a decade of Italian feminism, of the old motifs of revenging honour and of faked pregnancy as a means of securing marriage.

The feminist attack on the family is consequently an attack on dominant images of women that reinforce the notion of male superiority from within as well as from without. The enormous support for the divorce and abortion campaigns testified to a widespread sense of dissatisfaction with the legal–ecclesiastical system that encouraged the helplessness of women even within the supposedly supportive framework of the family. In the build-up to the divorce referendum in 1974 Christian Democrat propaganda insisted that women would be the force to 'hold the family together', yet in the final analysis it was women who provided the catalysing force for change. But the extent of the change is often difficult to measure and the complex nature of Italian feminism can be misleading to outsiders.

It must be remembered that in the south of Italy and in Sicily and Sardinia the condition of women has changed little since antiquity. Various writers have given us a terrifying picture of a closed world, in which a woman's horizons do not extend outside the confines of her own village and in which she can often reckon on living a life of grass widowhood, with a husband working in the north or abroad and a growing brood of small children to bring up single-handed.

The situation of the peasant woman left to cope with the after-effects of massive male emigration underwent a change in the years of rebuilding after the war. Italian industry expanded rapidly and hundreds of thousands of peasants crowded into the cities looking for work and for a chance to share in the prosperity being pedalled so enthusiastically by the new mass media. These peasants turned factory workers followed two basic patterns – either they left their womenfolk behind in the villages and thus stressed the division between town and country, or they brought families with them to settle in jerry-built suburbs and shanty towns on the outskirts. Gradually, the more fortunate workers moved upmarket to more prosperous flats and resolutely pushed their children towards the acquisition of a middle-class education. Elsewhere, peasants made fortunes overnight by selling land for building speculation, and in turn moved into the burgeoning cities.

The sudden increase in urban populations meant that large numbers of city dwellers were people whose roots in rural areas had been drastically torn out. Since in most cases the men worked and the women were left at home, what developed – and is still developing – was a family structure in which a whole range of different ideologies met. Children who grew up in moderate prosperity in an urban environment saw the world very differently from their parents or grandparents, who had been shaped by the rules of conduct for surviving in a world governed by the laws of nature.

The sexual revolution of the 1960s, translated into Italian terms, often meant the relaxing of certain rules of conduct that would have been intolerable to Anglo-Saxon youth two generations previously. As a student in Rome in the early 1960s I remember going with friends to night-clubs at five o'clock in the afternoon so that we could all be home by eight in time for the family dinner, leaving the evening session to married couples or those in search of loose living. By 1969 such habits were in decline, and by the 1980s friends' teenage daughters can go off freely to evening pop concerts. But one detail has not changed, has indeed been reinforced by the increased publicity given to violence against women, and that is the question of a woman's freedom of movement at night. It comes as a shock to British and American feminists to find Italian women still so enmeshed in the rituals of *accompagnamento* – the accompanying of women to and from their destination, whether by men or by other women. Again, it could be argued that the public transport system is inadequate and so the system of *accompagnamento* has inevitably grown, but the perpetuation of the system seems to derive much more from the notion of a lone woman as public property and hence at risk. The phenomenon of the large number of women drivers in Italy is closely linked to the question of freedom of movement without sexual harassment. The frustrations of dealing with lengthy traffic jams are preferable to being manhandled on crowded, inadequate public transport, and this has become quite acceptable to everyone. Jokes about the inadequacy of women as drivers are not standard in the Italian repertoire, and the British pattern of the husband who drives a car to a station so as to leave it for the day until he returns to collect it again, while the wife shops, works and organizes children on foot or on buses, is not a part of the daily Italian experience.

The campaigns against violence and the Reclaim the Night marches in Italy must therefore be seen in a very different social context from those in Britain and the USA. Italian women are not starting from the assumption that because male violence has increased the streets must be made safe again; they start from the premise that the free movement of a lone woman along a street, day or night, without verbal or physical interference is a prize indeed, because it has never been part of their experience. In the same way, the anti-pornography campaigns of Italian feminists must also be perceived rather differently. In Britain and the United States there is a clear point at which feminist feeling and a form of extreme right-wing puritanism can meet on the issue of the exploitation of sexuality through pornography. In Italy, the attitude of feminist groups to pornography is not so clear-cut.

In *Sorelle d'Italia* ('Sisters of Italy'), a study of images of women from 1968 to 1978, the organization of visual and textual material is very revealing. The book is divided into five sections: (1) 'La militante' ('The militant woman'); (2) 'La consumata' ('Woman as consumer product'); (3) 'La liberata' ('The emancipated woman'); (4) 'La creativa' ('The creative woman'); (5) 'La tradizionale' ('The traditional woman'). Each section contains photographs inset with extracts from a variety of textual sources – early documents of the women's movement in Section 1, excerpts from plays and poems in Section 4, extracts from women's magazines in Section 5 – and this material is framed within a series of interviews with leading Italian women – Dacia Maraini, writer and theatre director, Luciana Castellini of the PCI, Manuela Fraire, feminist theoretician, a leading Christian Democrat spokeswoman for Catholic unity, etc. Section 1 concludes with a series of images entitled 'feminist violence' – two photographs of women on protest marches, a photograph of the 1976 occupation of Milan cathedral by women shrouded in hoods and scarves and a double-page spread of a young, masked woman guerilla. Immediately after this, Section 2 opens with an interview with Leonora Fani, an actress who has appeared in box-office pornographic movies, one of which featured her having intercourse with a large dog. Leonora Fani defends her work with the now traditional 'they don't have to see it if they don't want to', line and the rest of Section 2 consists of an extraordinary set of pornographic photos, depicting various aspects of brutalized sex and of half-naked female bodies taken from advertising, the cinema and magazines both for men and for a general readership. The effect of this organization is to draw direct links between the determination of feminists to organize in violent protest against a society capable of producing such images and the acquiescence of readers in the development of such a state of affairs. The whole question of pornography, in short, has become politicized. What is under attack is not the fact of pornography but its implications – the use it makes of woman as a product and the way in which it reinforces the dominant ideological structure. Maria Rosa Cutrufelli shows how sexuality and the family are inevitably linked and points to the heart of the case against pornography:

No feminist organization (before the Second World War) had dared to radically attack the sexual relationship, which in its present cultural dimension is the central core of women's oppression. A sexual relationship is first and foremost a relationship between people, and hence social. Being a relationship between socially distinguished human beings, it is a political relationship. But it is also above all a relationship of production and in that sense it is regulated and controlled by the institution of the family. From here, from the sexual relationship and the family as fundamental points for the safeguarding of oppression, comes the capitalist plan to order the exploitation of women.[12]

The Italian women's movement, as part of its struggle to find a power base and a language, has not hesitated to produce counter-pornography, albeit of an ironic nature. Comic-strip stories describing the inadequacies of men in bed, deliberately mocking the pornographic comics for men in which women are raped and abandoned by well-endowed males, started to appear in the 1970s. The deliberately ugly graphics of magazines like *Strix*, for example, show women in dominant sexual positions, deserting and humiliating men, reversing the standard images of this kind of comic.

The politicization of such tracts is clear from the outset, and the title page of *Strix*, no. 2 (February 1979), contained a statement of solidarity with the women at Radio Donna attacked by gunmen in the studios a few days earlier:

All solidarity with the sisters of Collettivo Casalinghe and Radiotre of Rome, struck down by fascists at the moment when priests and police are trying to push back our fight any way they can.

What this kind of writing seeks to do is to deny the convention that allows pornography to present women as deviant and therefore exploitable. It goes together with an attempt by a number of feminist writers to 'liberate' terminology previously used by men – the Italian equivalent of four-letter words have entered women's vocabularies, and the old norms governing the use of such language are being violated. The notion of woman as gentle and maternal, set apart from struggle and vulgarity, which fascist ideology posited, is countered by the crude language and violent behaviour of the heroines of the new feminist comic strip.

Yet underlying this attempt to take over forms of speech previously denied to women is a premise that links such writing to the more widely known work of writers such as Natalia Ginzburg, Elsa Morante and Dacia Maraini: the search for a new language in which to express women's condition. This is the point at which several strands of the Italian women's movement run together, and theory and practice unite in a common concern with the problem of language and power relations. In 1978 Marina Yaguello declared:

the struggle for equality, for freedom, for cultural identity implies, for women as for all oppressed groups, minorities, deviant or small scale groups, the battle for the right to expression, to words, for the right to define themselves and determine themselves . . . [13]

Dacia Maraini has suggested that the slogans devised and utilized by the Italian women's movement are part of the new search for an individualistic creativity, and she places the slogans together with poetry and theatre. This may seem to be a rather sweeping claim, but it is certainly the case that feminist slogans in Italy have added a new dimension to the language. 'Donna è bello' represents a clear attempt to reformulate the basic rules of grammar in order to break down the old categories of masculine and feminine. As with the 'liberating' of obscenities, the assault on grammatical gender suggests that women are trying to widen the discussion not only to how language functions but also whose it is.

The proliferation of theoretical works on language and women is further evidence of this trend in Italian thought. But whereas the language debate in English-speaking countries has focused on the sexism implicit in syntactical and semantic structures, in Italy the emphasis is more theoretical and focuses on the idea of a separate language of women. Arguing that language is male-determined and therefore that creative arts based in language are also male-determined, women have made various suggestions for an alternative vision of creativity. What is still a fairly rudimentary debate in English-speaking countries as to the meaning of the term 'women's writing' (*for* or *by* women, or both?) is a highly complex debate in Italy, as well as in France, which has led feminist semioticians to posit a theory of an alternative creativity that merely leaves a 'trace' in existing texts and remains uncategorized. The question asked by theoreticians like Michel Foucault and Jacques Derrida as to what constitutes an author's work – i.e., can we describe everything written by an author as part of his or her 'work', including laundry lists – has special relevance when applied to a consideration of women's writing, since so much of women's activity within the structure of the family involves the composition of letters for school, shopping lists, instructions to helpers etc. And the terminological problem of distinguishing between 'female, feminist and women's creativity' takes on new complexities in Italian, in which different values are associated with the terms *femminile* (feminine), *femminista* (feminist) and *donna* (woman). Again, it is possible to link the proliferation of this kind of work to trends in Italian intellectual life, whereas in the Anglo-American world there has never been a tendency towards theoretical debate.

The connection between an alternative theory of women's creativity and the praxis of the women's movement in Italy returns us to the question of silent participation. If women are perceived as the silent army of resistance in wartime, as the silent revolutionaries who voted divorce into the Italian constitution, as the majority of the population (in Italy women outnumber men) with a minute, almost silent voice in parliament (out of 952 representatives in both houses in 1980, there were fifty-two women deputies and ten senators), it is easy to see how the theory of neglect of women's creativity might appeal. According to this notion, women's talk, gossip and the exchange of recipes and information about children, diaries and occasional autobiographical pieces are all part of that alternative creativity that has passed unseen, undervalued or even despised for centuries. If the dominant discourse were not male, with a particular forward-looking concept of time and a desire for immortality through artefacts, then gossiping, knitting, letter-writing, love stories and household diaries might have been perceived as eminently desirable forms of creativity. Or, to put it another way, the dichotomy between personal and political taken up as a rallying cry by the international women's movements might never have been perceived as a dichotomy at all.

After 1977, the year in which the Italian communist party made its 'historic compromise', as it came to be known, with the groups of the centre Right, and after urban terrorism reached the crisis point with the assassination of Aldo Moro, Italian feminist writing began to change its emphasis. Now the term in use was *dopofemminismo* (post-feminism), a specifically Italian concept on a level with the notion of post-structuralism. In an article entitled 'Provaci ancora, donna' ('Try again, woman') that appeared in *La Repubblica*, 30 May 1980, Maria Antonietta Macchiocchi claimed that feminist movements emerged in the wake of larger revolutionary movements. She argued that in 1789 and again in 1848, women of all classes were actively banding together and urging the discussion of specifically women's ideas. She traced this line of thought through the role played by women in the Paris Commune of 1870, the bolshevik revolution, and the various struggles of the twentieth century down to the cultural revolution of 1968, and went on to attack what she called 'marxist mystification of the emancipation of women', denying that there were close links between a socialist concept of revolution and a feminist one. She concluded:

The great drinking bout is over. The confrontation feminist is going home. She can sit down, put her banners and placards away and think over her own affairs with some anguish. She is re-evaluating the private. One day they will ask us how this story of feminism ended, how it happened that such a frenzy of hope could be followed by an indifference close to nihilism. But this preface must conclude with an attempt at a reply, with the belief that there will indeed be a liberation movement not *for* women but *caused* by women. A change spread across the personal life of a woman passes into the private. After the death of institutionalized feminism there will be a molecular reorganization, invisible from the outside, of behaviour, of sensuality, of contact with one's own body, of words themselves. A subtle impalpable net will be spread beneath which a new female revolt will be released by other means. Nothing will be forgotten under the experimental armour-plating of character erected in recent years. Only women have known how to safeguard inside themselves that which the dominating power of men crushes in human beings: the imperceptible personal freedom in the face of day-to-day hierarchy.

Maria Antonietta Macchiocchi's rather florid, slightly mystical style reveals a feeling in common with other feminists of various political persuasions that the first period of feminism has come to an end. Dacia Maraini has explained how her work in theatre has progressed from the 'theatre of the barricades' to a more complex concept that may not necessarily appear to be overtly feminist in character. And, writing in a special issue of *Differenze* on politics in November 1979, Michi Staderini declared that 'No one is talking about revolution any more on the "revolutionary" Left and no one is talking about "liberation" in the various women's movement groups.' She relates this change directly to the increased violence of the 1970s and to a changing concept of revolution in favour of a notion of mass insurrection. But she also feels that the feminist movement has contributed greatly to these changes by forcing a re-evaluation of the relationship between revolutionary men on the Left and women, and then by showing the contradictions and differences that can exist among women with different aims. The central problem, she believes, lies in the *rapporto tra individuo–collettivo* ('relationship between individual–collective'):

At first the aim of the collectives and the older forms of feminism seemed like the same liberation to us, even though they had not always been so for everyone. Individually they helped lift a great weight, but they did not always mean greater self-awareness for all women . . .

The great hopes of the early movement have ended, for Michi Staderini and for Maria Antonietta Macchiocchi, in a certain bitterness. And in the article that sets out the theory of post-feminism, 'Dopo il femminismo' ('After feminism'), that sense of dissatisfaction is summed up:

It is time to disentangle ourselves from the certainties on which we built feminism and ordered our daily privacy. Repression. Passivity. Inferiority. Femininity. Standing on the sidelines. Absence. Against all that, vindicating ourselves. Equality. Participation. Discourse. Sexuality. Pleasure. Fullness. It is time to wipe out the feminism that has been a long series of questions already inscribed in the answers. Feminism, the female's capital, needed the woman problem to present itself and define itself, draped in the cloth she so skilfully wove to hide all that which is unrepresentable and indefinable, i.e. the symptom of the emptiness of every possible relationship or human contract.[14]

The Italian women's movement of the post-feminist phase seems to be moving towards a more introspective position against a background of increased violence in society as a whole, involving women in particular, both as victims and as perpetrators. But the re-evaluation process in no way implies a slackening of interest in the problems of women or a lack of awareness; rather, it implies a depth of perception of the complexity of the issues which render earlier solutions impossibly naive. Once the shouting of the mass rallies died down, Italian feminists began the task of investigating the meaning of such paradoxical combinations as power and silence, personal and political, past and present. It is interesting to note that when the new women's university was set up in Rome the most popular course was Greek literature, showing the extent of a desire to explore the origins of Western culture and practice. The need for *contestazione* (protest through challenge) has given way to analysis of the basis of culture and society.

The impact of the women's movement in Italy has been far-reaching. The early rallies brought hundreds of thousands of women into the streets. The success of the divorce campaign, together with the number of women prepared to state publicly that they had had abortions, brought out into the open sensitive issues that had been hidden for years. During the 1970s there was an astonishing proliferation of feminist writing, the setting up of a daily newspaper, *Quotidiano donna*, and the advent of free broadcasting and local radio and television stations run by women. The collapse of the traditional alliance with the Left served to politicize and to focus attention on the women's movement, and in rejecting the construct of 'feminist' the most recent Italian post-feminist work seems to be moving towards what can only be described as a new philosophy.

But perhaps the best indication of the effects of feminism in Italy can be found in the changes in popular women's magazines. Even the traditionally conservative ones like *Grazia* testify to the differences in consciousness, with a move away from the old value system of the virgin and madonna as the desirable symbols of aspiration for all right-minded women. And what clearer evidence of the development of political consciousness than an article which appeared in 1979 in *Amica* (which together with *Annabella* has always tended to be more liberal than other Italian women's magazines) entitled 'Le compagne scoprono di essere donne' ('The women comrades discover they are women'). In this article, four books on the role of women within the Italian communist party are reviewed and questions are put that go to the heart of the crisis in the alignment of the women's movement with the Left. What are 'women comrades', asks the article, and are they men or women? What did it cost them to get into politics? And for whom are they involved in politics at all – for the party or for women in general? The article explains the differences between communist women of an earlier generation who came into the party because of family links and who were involved in the struggle against fascism, and the younger generation, who are disillusioned with their male comrades and who are trying to restructure the party from within. This is the other face of *dopofemminismo*, of women continuing to act in the public arena but on totally different assumptions from before. The author quotes Danis Frigato, a party member from the Venice area writing in *Care compagne*:

We have to measure ourselves by politics, which is often an abstract science in Italy that has very little to do with people's real needs. And in fact we are more aware because we suffer more, we pay a higher price for being women . . . For myself, I live in this awareness all the time. I haven't got married and I don't intend to. This isn't the choice of an old militant communist who has devoted herself body and soul to the party and given up the idea of a family. Nowadays the ideal woman worker *ought* to have a husband, probably even a child. I don't want any of that. I can't imagine a relationship with a man that isn't full of conflict. Separatism is a price that our generation has to pay. Even with my male comrades there's constant conflict and I've accepted that by now as inevitable.

This statement by a communist woman shows how far the move towards a specifically women's concept of politics has been taken in Italy, for, although she has chosen to operate within party structures, her attitude is closer to that of someone like Maria Antonietta Macchiocchi in stressing the need for internal revaluation and a refusal of male-determined goals.

Italian feminism may look rather strange to the British or American observer. Beautifully dressed women, accompanied by men to restaurants where they sit and discuss high-level theories of female consciousness, may seem a betrayal of the early cries for an alliance between women and workers as mutually oppressed social groups. Quiet teenage girls who take part, perhaps only once, in a Red Brigade kidnapping attempt and then return to their homes as if nothing had ever happened hardly fit the image of the new feminist-guerilla stereotype. But then the great lesson to be learned from the Italian feminist experience is that the stereotyped image of the 'active feminist' is as much a male construct as any other image of women. The grammatical conundrum of 'Donna è bello' is a revolutionary statement of radical dimensions because it challenges the very nature of structured language itself, and this slogan is the Italian hub of the wheel whose spokes may be made up of feminist thought and practice but whose outer circle is Italian women as a whole.

Notes

1   M. Daly, *Gyn/Ecology* (London: The Women's Press, 1979), p. 216.

2   M. R. Cutrufelli, *L'invenzione della donna: Miti e tecniche dello sfruttamento* (The Invention of Women: Myths and Techniques of Exploitation) (Milan: Mazzotta, 1974), pp. 47–8. Throughout the chapter, English quotations from articles or books published in Italian or French are my own translations.

3   M. A. Macchiocchi, 'Female sexuality in fascist ideology', *Feminist Review*, vol. 1 (1979), pp. 68–9.

4   J. Bowlby, author of *Maternal Care and Mental Health* (1952), put forward the notion that women who worked deprived their children of necessary love and care during their formative years. His views coincided with a wider campaign to persuade women to return to the home, vacating places in the labour market to the large number of demobbed men waiting for work.

5   Quoted in R. Rossanda, *Le altre* (The Others), transcripts of Radiotre interviews (Milan: Bompiani, 1979), p. 67.

6   Quoted in E. Scroppo, *Donna, privato e politico* (Woman, the Private and the Political) (Milan: Mazzotta, 1979), p. 26.

7   Scroppo, *Donna*, p. 29.

8   Scroppo, *Donna*, p. 67.

9   *Sputiamo su Hegel* appeared in several different versions. One is reproduced in R. Spagnoletti, *I movimenti femministi in Italia* (Rome: Savelli, 1978), pp. 107–36.

10 G. Pomata, *In scienza e coscienza: donna e potere nella società borghese* (In Knowledge and Awareness: Women and Power in Bourgeois Society) (Bologna: La Nuova Italia, 1979), p. 19.

11 Pomata, *Scienza e coscienza*, p. 16.

12 Cutrufelli, *L'invenzione della donna*, pp. 122–3.

13 M. Yaguello, *Les Mots et les Femmes* (Paris: Payot, 1978), p. 195.

14 P. Alberti and R. Mangaroni, 'Dopo il femminismo', *Il cerchio di gesso* (after-feminism) (1977–78), pp. 55–9.

Chapter Four

Britain

Analysing the development of the women's movement in Britain is an almost impossible task. At first glance, the British tradition of feminism appears to offer a flourishing example of women's power and influence from the eighteenth century onwards. From Mary Wollstonecroft, pioneer feminist, to Elizabeth Fry, Quaker prison reformer, to Elizabeth Garrett Anderson, prime mover in the struggle to establish the credibility of women in the medical profession, the map of British history is peopled with similarly determined female individualists. Today, feminist bookshops throughout the world are stocked with works by Virginia Woolf and Dora Russell, Doris Lessing and the Brontës, and with studies of the suffragettes and of the contributions of women like the Pankhursts to social and political life. Yet when we look behind that list of famous names, a picture emerges that calls into question the very existence of a feminist tradition in British life that reaches any but a restricted, middle-class few.

As with all aspects of British life, the fundamental structures of society are based on archaic and rigid notions of class. The growth of the Welfare State since the Second World War has led to assumptions about the changing nature of the class system, and it must be acknowledged that to some extent changes have taken place. What has not changed, however, is the reliance of British society on class as a crucial factor in its health and education systems, in its legal system, and in its business world, Symbolically, the upper chamber of the British parliament, the House of Lords, is filled with hereditary peers whose family backgrounds rather than training or special skills, have placed them in this key political position.

From outside, the British class system is inexplicable. From inside, it is amorphous, constantly shifting, but immensely powerful, exerting pressure on all aspects of British life. Accents, table manners, schools, newspapers, clothes, opinions, even choice of family pet, all reveal clues, to anyone trained to read minute signs, as to the class position of an individual. To an observer not trained to read those signs, the distinctions are imperceptible. The heavy boots, headscarf and ill-fitting coat worn by the Queen in the country could equally be seen among the tents at Greenham Common. The dirty, ragged Indian carpet on the floor of an Oxford professor's house might not be read as a sign of nonchalant class superiority but perhaps as a testimony to poverty. The perfect rounded vowels of Margaret Thatcher appear to many to be the acme of educated speech – only an ear trained in the refinements of British accents can distinguish the regional lower-class voice still trapped inside the decorative shell of RP (received pronunciation).

Attempting, then, to look at the many faces of British feminism, one becomes enmeshed in the problems caused by the pervasive nature of the class system. The debate between black and white feminists, already familiar in the United States, is exacerbated in Britain by the implacable hostility of many working-class feminists to the middle classes. At the same time, the anti-intellectualism which prevails in British society contributes another layer of confusion, since many of the better-known women in British feminism are university-educated, a sign of privilege accorded to a minuscule percentage of the overall population. Moreover, the picture is further blurred when the position of the Left in general is considered, since the strong lines of anti-feminist, indeed anti-female, tradition are still very apparent inside the trade union movement.

It is a common misconception that women in Catholic countries, where abortion, contraception and divorce were (and often still are) illegal, have found themselves in positions of greater inferiority than women in northern Europe. In fact, the comparison needs to be considered from a different angle. First, the illegality of what were perceived as essential rights of women enabled the women's movement in several countries in southern Europe to attract vast support across the social range. In the late 1960s and early 1970s huge divorce and abortion campaigns drew together women from all walks of life in mass protests, something that has happened rarely and with difficulty in Britain, where protests have tended to be on a smaller scale and frequently based in London. Moreover, the women's movements in Catholic countries of southern Europe have had to grapple with the tradition of the dual image of woman as Holy Mother and Whore, the double-sided view of women that is both positive and negative, since the idea of mother-veneration is not altogether disadvantageous to women.

In Britain, where there is no tradition of mother-veneration, the picture is very different. Moreover, linked to the absence of any idealized image of woman in British society is a parallel lack of child idealization. Women and children are unwelcome in all kinds of contexts in public life, from working-men's clubs and billiard halls, to gentlemen's clubs and wine bars. A classic example of the devaluation of women and children was provided in the summer of 1983, when a small girl won a competition intended primarily for boys, of which the prize was a seat in the all-male commentator's box at Lord's Cricket Ground.

In spite of her achievement, and in spite of the rules of the competition, the child was denied a seat in the masculine enclave. British newspapers are regularly filled with similar stories, used as fillers between stories of larger national and international interest. The slow penetration of women into professions previously exclusively male has also received extensive media coverage. From the first woman employed in the Stock Exchange to the first woman bus driver, from the first woman station master (*sic*) to the first woman National Hunt jockey, all these women have been treated as prodigies and given media attention. The first woman newsreader became a national figure, the first woman to sail round the world could command a six-figure fee for an unwritten first novel. It is difficult to imagine this kind of media treatment of similar events anywhere else in Europe, where women have been employed in all walks of life for so long that the surprise value has ceased to exist.

Hostility in public places towards small children and women, astonishment at women's professional ability, resentment shown by government ministers and the writers of letters to local newspapers at women working in times of high unemployment, all testify to the prevalence of sexist attitudes in British society right across the political spectrum. British popular newspapers carry daily pin-up photos of naked 'girls', and in 1979 the left-wing paper the *Yorkshire Miner* attempted to boost its sales by the use of pin-ups, and vigorously defended this action despite the protests of women trade unionists. The presentation of images of women as desirable bodies appeared to offer no difficulty to men on the British Left, any more than to men on the British Right.

It is perhaps typical of the conflicting forces in British society that, while so-called family newspapers promote an image of women as sexual objects, in other areas British life is puritanical .and repressive. Four-letter words are still bleeped out on television and corporal punishment is still tolerated in schools in spite of appeals to the European Court of Human Rights. Beneath the ordered surface of British society, the levels of violence against women and children remain probably the worst in the Western world.

If the picture of British social life so far presented has been somewhat bleak, it is nevertheless important to depict that bleakness to counter the common misconception that British women have somehow enjoyed greater freedom than their European and American sisters and are today in a position of privilege. Those women who were and are in positions of public prominence owe their status not so much to their sex as to their abilities to operate to advantage within the class system, and perhaps no one figure illustrates the difficulties involved in trying to isolate feminism from class-consciousness so much as Margaret Thatcher, the first British woman Prime Minister.

The response of British feminists to Thatcher has been uncompromisingly antagonistic, a fact which American feminists find difficult to comprehend. Although the election of a woman to high public office was perceived by many US feminists as a positive gesture, British feminists saw only the fundamental anti-feminism of Thatcher's political position. Significantly, in 1979 there was an overall drop-in the number of women Members of Parliament, and Thatcher's advisers and Cabinet colleagues have remained almost exclusively male. Moreover, it has been amongst the Conservative government under Thatcher that voices have begun to question the right of women to work at all. Arguing for the need to keep as many men in employment as possible, the government has raised the old chestnut about women's true role being in the family, though the irony of such views being expressed by a government led by a woman who is the mother of two children does not seem to have been noticed.

In spite of her male entourage, Margaret Thatcher has continued to promote an image of her own womanliness, giving interviews to women's magazines about her domestic interests and her children's problems, insisting on the special capacities of women to get things done. 'We have a much more practical approach', she is quoted as saying in *Woman's Own*, 17 October 1981, 'and in the end it's often the women who are left to cope with all the practical problems. We can't ignore them, we can't get round them.' And without doubt, she appeals to a high percentage of women in Britain: a *New Statesman* poll just before the 1979 election showed 55 per cent of women preparing to vote Conservative, as opposed to only 51 per cent of men. Her blend of populist views on larger issues such as capital punishment, privatization, law and order, and, of course, since the Falklands War, defence spending, with a traditionalist view of womanhood have contributed to her popularity. She is a mother who cares for her children, dresses quietly but tastefully, never swears, drinks or loses self-control, and brings together a set of virtues that cut across class lines by idealizing bourgeois woman. It should never be forgotten that English is a language that makes a clear social distinction between *women* and *ladies*. You are born as one, you aspire to be the other, but only a few are chosen. Some, the privileged minority, are born into the class that defines them as 'ladies'. Margaret Thatcher stands as an example of a woman born into a class that aspired to rise above itself, and in her constant insistence on her humble origins she ensures that this part of her life story is not forgotten by men or women alike. In the *Woman's Own* interview she repeats the details of how her father left school at 13, thereby missing the educational opportunities that should have been his, leaving her to live out the father's dream:

When I went to Oxford it was the opportunity of my life. I was unbelievably grateful to have it. My son was offered a place at Oxford. And he had a year between school and university. But he came to the conclusion that university was not for him. He wanted to go and start doing things. Eventually he went to the City of London to get a foundation course in accountancy. Now all that happened in three generations. University – undreamed of for my father. My dream. My son's refusal. That has happened in this country in *three* generations.

Born a woman, Margaret Thatcher has become a lady. Her success story is not the tale of a *woman* who rises to power, but of a person from the *petite bourgeoisie* who crossed the class lines, in precisely the same way as those lionized working-class musicians and business tycoons who broke out of their class enclave in the economic climate of the 1960s. Elected to Parliament as a substitute for her husband, Nancy Astor played up her femininity because she was sure of her class position from the outset. Sixty years later, unsure of her class position, Margaret Thatcher stresses her womanliness, her domesticity, in newspaper interviews, while playing the power game on the same terms as the men around her.

Margaret Thatcher's concern with her public image, and the media attention to that image, presented feminists with another dilemma. A remark like Julian Critchley's in his *Times* profile of Margaret Thatcher – 'She cannot see an institution without hitting it with her handbag' –[1] is easily perceived as offensively sexist, as were the many references to her clothes and hairstyle in public appearances immediately before and after the 1979 election. That she was singled out for particularly sexist sniping in the press, and that attention was given to her appearance in a manner unprecedented among male politicians, caused problems for those feminists opposed to such sexist behaviour while also disapproving of Conservative policies. And there was anger amongst women at the way in which Thatcher's sex was used against her by the opposition. Fightback for Women's Rights, a feminist campaign started within the Labour Party in 1980, sent an open letter to trade unions stating:

Sexist abuse such as bitch, cow and other less printable epithets make many women trade unionists feel that they are outsiders in a movement that has such feelings of hatred towards Thatcher purely as a woman.

Attacking Thatcher for her policies had led to attacks on her as a woman, and this has created the ironic situation in which female trade unionists have felt that they had to defend her against their own comrades who had blurred the lines between political criticism and sexist abuse. In this, as in the case of the pin-ups in the *Yorkshire Miner*, the depths of anti-feminism, indeed anti-female feeling, on the Left were being plumbed.

The defence of Thatcher by Labour women also reveals the curious way in which image and appearance are linked to class relations in British life. Whereas in North America and in Europe, class is more closely tied to material wealth, in Britain clothes, like nuances of accent and taste in furniture, speak volumes. Margaret Thatcher's style, if such it can be called, is a stylelessness that accords with a notion of classlessness. Interviewed in *Woman's Own* in 1976, she announced that high fashion did not interest her, but 'I believe that if you look good, people warm to you'. Sentiments close to those of Ray Strachey who, when discussing the efforts of feminists in the 1880s, noted that 'when an audience expected to find a fierce and strident virago, and found instead a young lady whose voice, dress and manner were not only quiet but exquisite, then indeed they were startled to attention'.[2] Looking nice is therefore equated with all kinds of inner virtues, and the notion of what constitutes 'exquisiteness' is one of balance – not too showy, not too rich, not too fashionable, something that will comfort all classes, will make all kinds of people warm to one.

Ray Strachey further criticized those women 'who did not realize at all that other people were given to judging by appearances', and whose arguments might be unconvincing 'if presented by a lady in thick boots, untidy hair and a crumpled dress'. Expressed in the 1920s, her views prefigure the views of the media who made much of the apparent unfashionableness of the women of Greenham Common, termed the '*ladies* of Greenham Common' by both the gutter press and the BBC, a terminological usage that carries a wealth of irony.

For British women, propriety of dress and decorous behaviour were seen as highly important issues throughout the nineteenth and twentieth centuries and are linked to the desirability of middle-class values in an industrial, colonizing society. The need for British feminists, at least in the early years of the women's movement, to reject the image of ladylike respectability demanded by middle-class mores is something that should therefore not be underestimated. Only the aristocracy, who perceive themselves as being above class strictures, have traditionally dressed to suit themselves, so, by establishing the right to a feminist image, even though risking the impression of creating a feminist uniform, British women have actually been challenging expectations established on the basis not only of sex but also of class.

Perhaps one of the most obvious demonstrations of the inferior position of British women lies in the extraordinary fact that an Equal Pay Act was not passed until 1970 and did not come into force until 1975. Moreover, as Anna Coote and Beatrix Campbell point out in their book *Sweet Freedom: The Struggle for Women's Liberation*, this legislation did not change women's unequal status in the fields of taxation and social security. The authors note that by 1981 women 'still had scarcely any more financial or legal independence than they had enjoyed in International Women's Year [1975]... Men continued to dominate the higher paid and skilled jobs and in 1980 they were still taking home, on average, 36 per cent more pay than women.'[3] It is hardly surprising that a society which took so long to institutionalize the concept of equal pay for equal work should also take a long time in putting the law into effective practice. Moreover, the vagueness of the Sex Discrimination Act which came into force with the Equal Pay Act left so many legal loopholes that anyone set against implementing the Act could manage to do so with relative impunity, a fact borne out by the difficulty women have had in winning cases of sex discrimination in employment. The Act differentiated between *direct* and *indirect* sex discrimination, a distinction spelled out by the Equal Opportunities Commission's *Short Guide to the Sex Discrimination Act 1975* in the following terms:

Direct discrimination involves treating a woman less favourably than a man because she is a woman.

Indirect discrimination means that conditions are applied which favour one sex more than the other but which cannot be justified. For example, if an employer, in recruiting clerks, insists on candidates being six feet tall, a case may be made that he is unlawfully discriminating.[4]

Despite the temptation to ridicule the looseness of the definitions, it should not be forgotten that the Act marked a genuine milestone in the unhappy story of women's labour rights in British society, a history of exploitation and undervaluation running parallel to the history of industrial development and colonial expansion overseas. It is perhaps significant that one of the most heavily exploited groups of manual workers in Britain today is that of Asian women. These women often have scanty knowledge of the English language, let alone knowledge of British customs and their rights as workers, and are therefore often employed without contracts on a part-time or temporary basis. Frequently underpaid and non-unionized, they have little or no redress against unfair dismissal and working conditions. Where these women are concerned, a range of prejudices combine to further discrimination against them: class prejudice, racism and sexism are combined with the low status of working-class Asian women in their ethnic community groups. Asian women have moved into the position occupied earlier this century by Irish and Jewish immigrants, employed in those jobs that native-born white workers despise.

In 1790 when Mary Wollstonecroft wrote *A Vindication of the Rights of Women*, she pointed out the equation of capitalism with the oppression of women:

The preposterous distinctions of rank, which render civilization a curse by dividing the world between voluptuous tyrants and cunning envious dependents, corrupt, almost equally, every class of people, because respectability is not attached to the discharge of the relative duties of life, but to the station, and when the duties are not fulfilled the affections cannot gain sufficient strength to fortify the virtue of which they are the natural reward. Still there are some loopholes out of which a man may creep, and dare to think and act for himself, but for a woman it is a herculean task, because she has difficulties peculiar to her sex to overcome which require almost superhuman powers.[5]

Described by Horace Walpole as a 'hyena in petticoats', she wrote as a believer in the intrinsic value of women, whom she felt were unjustly treated in English society, and as a believer in the power of enlightened education to make good that discrimination. For her, the French Revolution acted as a catalyst and, in common with a number of French and English female freethinkers, she passionately argued the case for intrinsic equality amongst all races, classes and sexes. She presents the reader with a series of powerful images – the waste of talent and energy when women are deprived of education, the unhealthy effects of a tyrannical, paternalistic father on the family, the horrors of venereal disease brought into the home by a philandering husband. Both in her theoretical writings and in her fiction, she makes a sound, deeply urged case, and one feels that, had she not been cut off tragically in childbirth, she would have been able to establish a much wider base of support for her views.

As it was, she was virulently attacked during her lifetime and has been the subject of ridicule and abuse ever since. Much of the abuse has been directed at her private life – her supposed immorality as manifested in her love affairs, her refusal to marry William Godwin, her children by different fathers. Wollstonecroft's attempts to live her life according to her ideals have been read as neurotic, irresponsible behaviour, and the very passion with which she expressed her views has come to be interpreted as a sign of emotional instability. In a book entitled *Modern Woman: The Lost Sex*, Ferdinand Lundberg and Marynia Farnham analyse Mary Wollstonecroft in scathing terms:

Mary Wollstonecroft hated men. She had every personal reason possible known to psychiatry for hating them. Hers was hatred of creatures she greatly admired and feared . . . Mary Wollstonecroft's life reads like a psychiatric case history. So, for that matter, do the lives of many later feminists . . . [She] was afflicted with a severe case of penis envy . . . that she was an extreme neurotic of a compulsive type there can be no doubt. Out of her illness arose the ideology of feminism, which was to express the feelings of so many women in years to come.[6]

The savagery of this attack is by no means unusual, and the abuse directed at Mary Wollstonecroft has been matched by the press treatment of later suffrage campaigners in the nineteenth century, and by the portrayal of the Greenham Common women in the media in the 1980s. Part of this attack is to suggest that a woman who asserts a claim to rights defined in her terms is somehow deranged, at best disturbed and always physically unattractive, implying that feminism is a surrogate for male suitors. Only ugly women, runs the myth, need draw attention to themselves through feminist activities; the more attractive women rely on their own sexuality and live fulfilled lives.

Yet what Mary Wollstonecroft proposed regarding the education and treatment of women was hardly revolutionary. In common with other radical thinkers of her age, she argued that human character was mainly formed by the environment, and proposed a programme of social and educational changes that would ameliorate the position of deprived groups in society, including, of course, women. Yet, as Sheila Rowbotham and others have pointed out, Mary Wollstonecroft's theories were limited in their radicalism: *The Vindication* does not show the means of achieving the social revolution it proclaims, and remains a work that considers the plight of middle-class women:

The Vindication, often taken as the beginnings of feminism, was rather the important theoretical summation of bourgeois radical feminism still in the phase of moral exhortation, before there was either the possibility of a radical and socialist movement from below, to which the revolutionary feminist could relate, or a movement like that of suffragettes, of privileged women for equal rights with bourgeois man.[7]

Throughout the nineteenth century, bourgeois feminism emerged in a variety of ways. Running alongside the various Reform Bills from the 1830s onwards were campaigns to change the laws of property and inheritance relating to women. In 1839, following the passionate campaigning of Caroline Norton (whose husband had refused her access to her children after their separation), the Infants' Custody Act passed into law. This Act established the right of a judge to award custody to mothers against whom adultery was not proven of children under the age of 7, with right of access to other children; but full equal guardianship of children did not come into effect until 1925. Linked to campaigns for establishing the rights of mothers were equally hard-fought campaigns for divorce reform and for the rights of married women to own property. As early as 1855, Barbara Leigh Smith managed to get a Married Women's Property Reform Bill as far as the House of Commons, but it was only in 1870 that a vastly truncated bill was passed. Effectively, this bill which allowed women to keep possession of anything they earned for themselves, was toothless in the extreme, since everything else continued to belong to husbands, regardless of whether it had been acquired before or after marriage, and these defects were not fully redressed until the 1920s.

Underlying the failure of so many proposals to improve the social and economic position of women in the nineteenth century were inadequate educational facilities and lack of voting rights. Writing in 1859 after her experiences in the Crimean War, Florence Nightingale attacked what she perceived as the stupidity and limitations of women in general, but pointed also to a cause: 'Very few people lead such an impoverishing and confusing and weakening life as the women of the richer classes.'[8] Other women, perhaps less cynical than Florence Nightingale, turned their similar impressions into action. In 1848 and 1849 respectively, Queen's College and Bedford College for Ladies were opened, and from the 1860s onwards there were struggles to establish women's colleges at Cambridge, with Emily Davies's founding of Girton College in 1873 the most striking success, although full membership of the university was not achieved by women until 1948. Elizabeth Garrett Anderson and Sophia Jex-Blake fought for the right of women to study medicine, a long drawn-out and bitter campaign. What does emerge from these varied struggles is the way in which individual middle-class women took on the task of fighting for specific goals. The history of the women's movement in the years between the death of Mary Wollstonecroft and the rise of the Pankhursts is peopled with individualists, often individualists who rejected any overt affiliations with feminism, and who frequently saw the roots of their struggles in philanthropy. Describing the women's movement as illuminated by the 'searchlight of the philanthropic movement' in the early nineteenth century, Ray Strachey lists a range of women, including Jane Austen, Mary Berry, Fanny Burney, Elizabeth Fry, Harriet Martineau and Mary Somerville, whom she terms 'true forerunners of the Women's movement', and between whom there existed a 'kind of freemasonry of understanding'.[9] But even when the idea of women's rights had begun to acquire some following, the women principally involved in attempts to change repressive family and divorce laws, to improve working conditions for poor women, to reform hospitals and prisons, and to widen professional and educational facilities for women, were primarily individualists who used their class position to exert influence on the system. It is important to bear in mind this individualist tradition, since it can be followed into our own times. Moreover, alongside this tradition, other kinds of feminist activity were beginning to take place.

In 1840 the World Anti-Slavery Conference was held in London, and the American delegation included four women who were not allowed to participate. Their exclusion so outraged them that on returning home they set about organizing another convention, to discuss the whole issue of women's rights, which was held at Seneca Falls in 1848. Nothing comparable happened in Britain, though there was an increase in women's organizational activities alongside the work of individual campaigners. Anne Knight, the Quaker abolitionist, who produced the first leaflet on women's suffrage around 1847, argued that the Chartist movement should take on the question of women's political rights, and groups of women workers began to organize with the trade unions. In 1876 at the Trades Union Congress a paper was presented by a woman on 'the organization of women's labour', and in 1888 the strike of women workers at Bryant & May's match factory resulted in union organization and some gains in improving working conditions.

But as Richard Evans points out in his study of liberal and

socialist feminist movements in the nineteenth century, even though industrialization was so far advanced in Britain, 'class collaboration had submerged the nascent labour movement in the liberal party'.[10] Socialism in Britain, he argues, was a 'fringe phenomenon' that only gradually moved into the forefront of the British political scene, and one line of early socialism was profoundly anti-feminist. In 1877 the secretary of the Trades Union Congress (TUC) parliamentary committee put the point of view of the majority of delegates to the Leicester TUC:

It was their duty as men and husbands to use their utmost efforts to bring about a condition of things, where their wives would be in their proper sphere at home, instead of being dragged into competition for livelihood against the great and strong men of the world.[11]

Traditionally, British socialism and feminism did not rest easily together. Nineteenth-century feminist activity, so deeply rooted in the upper middle class was remote from the aims of emergent socialism. The small organizations of working women founded in the nineteenth century predictably focused on the immediate problems of low wages and poor working conditions in industry, rather than on any larger, feminist issues. Bourgeois feminism remained philanthropic in its bias, and thus class lines were sharply drawn in ways that were to lead to the split in the Pankhurst suffrage campaign and to the division that still marks British feminism today.

In 1866 a petition was presented to Parliament by John Stuart Mill and Henry Fawcett demanding that the suffrage reforms being discussed should include votes for women. The failure of the petition led to the establishing of the National Society for Women's Suffrage in 1867, and a number of private bills were put forward over the next fifty years as part of a concerted campaign to keep the question of votes for women under public scrutiny. By 1897 some sixteen women's suffrage societies came together in the National Union of Women's Suffrage Societies, and by 1913 the number of societies represented had risen to 400. Richard Evans points to this growth of feminism as an indication of the strength of the British movement:

> Viewed in a European perspective, the British feminist movement was by the 1900s not only large and vigorous but also radical and successful. By 1910 its suffrage movement had become one of the biggest in the world . . . It had long enjoyed a degree of support in the legislature unparalleled even in America.[12]

Yet in spite of this strength, the practical results remained negligible. British parliamentary tactics successfully curtailed feminist activities, in spite of the huge campaigns for the women's cause of public meetings, civil actions, demonstrations and the support of public figures. And in speculating why this should have been the case, we should consider the question of the gap between middle-class, educated feminists on the one hand and women workers on the other. In 1906, Eva Gore-Booth, a radical suffragist whose support for the movement arose from her belief in the need for the vote as a means of improving labour relations, wrote to Mrs Fawcett, president of the National Union of Women's Suffrage Societies, to protest about the tactics of the suffragettes:

> There is no class in the community who has such good reasons for objecting and does so strongly object to shrieking and throwing yourself on the floor and struggling and kicking as does the average working woman, whose human dignity is very real to her. We feel we must tell you this for this reason that we are in great difficulties because our members in all parts of the country are so outraged at taking part in such proceedings, that everywhere for the first time they are shrinking from public demonstrations. It is not the fact of demonstrations or even violence that is offensive to them, it is being mixed up and held accountable as a class for educated and upper class women who kick, shriek, bite and spit. As far as importance in the eyes of the government goes, where shall we be if working women do not support us?[13]

In their book *One Hand Tied Behind Us*, Jill Liddington and Jill Norris have analysed the rise of the women's suffrage movement, and pay special attention to the role of working-class women's groups. They argue persuasively that media attention has always focused on the role of a small group of middle-class campaigners led by Emmeline Pankhurst and her daughter Christabel, and discuss the way in which the Pankhursts steadily alienated large numbers of women who had at first joined them in the Women's Social and Political Union (WSPU) which they had founded in 1903. When in 1912 Christabel had to escape to Paris to avoid imprisonment, Teresa Billington, a Manchester schoolteacher and early recruit to the WSPU wrote:

Daring to advertise in an unconventional way the movement has dared nothing more. It has cut down its demand from one of sex equality to one of votes on a limited basis. It has suppressed free speech on fundamental issues. It has gradually edged the working class element out of the ranks. It has become socially exclusive, punctiliously correct, gracefully fashionable, ultra-respectable and narrowly religious.[14]

The advent of the First World War changed the pattern of feminist politics. Christabel Pankhurst returned from Paris and, with her mother, offered her services to the nation, speaking out publicly in favour of the war effort. Gradually both women moved even further to the Right, with Mrs Pankhurst finally joining the Conservative Party and Christabel becoming a Dame Commander of the Order of the British Empire and ending her life as an advocate of the Second Coming of Christ. Only Sylvia, Christabel's sister, who had campaigned on a socialist platform in London's East End and had found herself expelled from the WSPU in 1914, remained true to her labour origins. For Sylvia, socialism and the women's cause were linked and had to be based on a strong working-class labour movement. Richard Evans comments that Sylvia Pankhurst, like Lily Braun in Germany, 'succeeded in crossing the barrier from bourgeois feminism to social democracy'.[15] The suffrage cause was finally won in 1918, when men were given the vote at 21 and women at the age of 30. Women also won the right to be candidates and the first woman Member of Parliament, Viscountess Astor, was elected in 1919, for the Conservatives. Not until 1928 was full adult suffrage granted, with men and women receiving equal voting rights from the age of 21.

After the war, feminism in Britain took a back seat. The apparent success of the suffrage campaign obscured the fact that women had been granted the vote due to their involvement in the war effort, and few voices raised the problem of the relationship between feminism and militarism, let alone between feminism and socialism. The women's movement had indeed been led down a road with a single-minded goal, and once that goal was reached there were no other destinations immediately in sight. Yet as early as 1920, in a review of a French book on the portrayal of women in English nineteenth-century fiction, Virginia Woolf commented wryly that:

Not even a woman and a Frenchwoman at that, looking with the clear-sighted eyes of her race across the Channel, can say for certain what the words 'emancipation' and 'evolution' amount to. Granted that the woman of the middle class has now some leisure, some education, and some liberty to investigate the world in which she lives, it will not be in this generation or in the next that she will have adjusted her position or given a clear account of her powers.[16]

In their book *Women, Power and Politics*, Margaret Stacey and Marion Price assume a similar position. The authors analyse the impact of the suffrage movement in a chapter tellingly entitled 'Suffrage without Emancipation', and show how so many of the women who entered Parliament in the 1920s did so only 'as surrogates for men or with bourgeois family support'.[17] Those women who succeeded in entering Parliament were either trading on the reputation already acquired by their menfolk, or were reliant on the power and influence of wealthy bourgeois family connections. In contrast, some of the Labour women who stood for Parliament in the period between 1918 and 1928 did not have such support, but it is significant that they were all single and able to pursue their political careers unhindered by the problems of child care. What Stacey and Price show, therefore, is that the entry of women into Parliament was due to a series of compromises – either they chose a career in politics and gave up family ambitions, or they relied on the groundwork being done by men and by the social status of their family.

Stacey and Price's work is important because they argue for a split in the relationship between women and power. The public arena of the workplace is seen as one power area for women, with the family representing a power base of a very different kind. Tracing the history of women's conquest of public areas of power in Britain over the past 150 years, they show that there has been some increase in the numbers of women actively involved in public life. The huge nineteenth-century campaigns did therefore result in certain changes, and women have steadily entered the professions and the educational system, though not in the numbers that might have been expected. On the other hand, in the family, women's power has diminished, an ironic result of increased male involvement in household tasks and the rearing of children. Stacey and Price conclude that 'the privatized nuclear family embedded in capitalist society maintains children's and women's lack of freedom', since women are isolated in small units, and that although women can enter the public world, they enter it 'at a disadvantage in terms of training and experience compared with their male peers who have been there continuously for many years'.[18]

The picture painted by Stacey and Price is disconcerting, since they show women losing out on two fronts: in the home, the traditional areas of power are being slowly whittled away, while in public life the prevailing strength of the class system ensures that very few women, and only those with strongly supportive families, are able to gain much ground. And when they come to relate these conclusions to recent feminist politics, the picture is downright gloomy. They conclude that in Britain upwardly mobile women have not been closely involved with the post-1968 feminist movement, and that the women's liberation movement in Britain has tended to be dominated by younger women uninvolved in public life.

Considering the evidence, I find it hard not to conclude that British women are doubly handicapped – by their sex, on the one hand, in common with women throughout the world, and by their place in the British class system, on the other. All too often, the class problem has led to confused thinking, a classic example of which was to be found in the June 1982 issue of *Spare Rib*, most widely read of monthly feminist magazines. In the spring of that year, the Conservative government, led by Margaret Thatcher, went to war with Argentina over territorial claims to the Falkland Islands. At the same time, Pope John Paul II became the first Pope since the Reformation to set foot on English soil. The Pope's visit was uncertain right up to the last minute because of the Falklands War, and when he finally arrived it was understood that he would proceed to visit Argentina immediately after visiting Britain, to stress his role as non-partisan peacemaker.

Spare Rib carried an editorial on both these events. The comments on the Falklands War were strongly anti-Thatcher, suggesting that like her Argentinian counterpart, General Galtieri, she had engineered the war to bolster her government's declining popularity and revive a spirit of jingoistic nationalism. In a final short paragraph the editorial attacked the attitude of the media to war, warning of the consequences to women in general:

The sickening media coverage of the 'boys going off to fight' while their girlfriends and mothers wait at home for their return would be reason enough for feminists to oppose the conflict. Lest *we* forget, war makes 'men' of boys, and 'girls' of women.

The second part of the editorial contained an attack on the Pope as 'the symbol of male power enshrined in religion', and called upon women to oppose the visit of so 'viciously anti-feminist' a man. But in making this appeal, the editors ran into problems. Having long since established an editorial line of supporting Roman Catholics in Northern Ireland, they must have seen that their supporters in the anti-Pope demonstration would be extremist Protestant groups, so while attacking the Pope's visit *per se*, they had to try to divorce their protest from that of groups most opposed to Irish unity. Struggling with this dilemma, the editorial proceeded to argue that, whilst opposing the Pope 'as a symbolic figure . . . we must also make it clear that we're giving no support for Protestant institutions – including the British government – that have created and used anti-Catholic prejudice for their own ends'.

When the two editorial comments are read together the obvious sincerity of the sentiments expressed comes across clearly, but so also does the confused political thinking. During his visit to Britain, the Pope became the most prominent public figure outside the committed anti-war Left to speak out against what was happening in the Falklands. Throughout his ten-day visit he made requests for peace in the South Atlantic; shortly afterwards, in Argentina, he reiterated the same message. Yet *Spare Rib* was asking women to ignore his role as peacemaker at the expense of his role as chief propagandist against contraception and abortion. It was a dilemma made all the more complex since the Pope directed his pleas for peace at one woman, Thatcher, standing at the epicentre of the warmongering crisis.

What the editors were asking of the readers was compartmentalized thinking. The Pope had to represent unequivocally male oppression, regardless of his anti-war stance, and Margaret Thatcher had to represent the fascist pro-war position in spite of her sex. At the same time, feminists were to dissociate themselves from those protestors against the Pope's visit who started from a differing ideological position. Such thinking was hopelessly undialectical, and came from a confusion of criteria, based on sex, class, party politics, religious views and pacificism.

The lack of dialectical thinking, of which the *Spare Rib* editorial is an extreme case, emerges time and time again in the presentation of controversial issues for British feminists. Yet as Sheila Rowbotham pointed out as early as 1973 in *Woman's Consciousness, Man's World*, women must constantly rethink their position in a highly complex global situation:

Theoretical consistency is difficult – often it comes out as dogmatism. It is hard to steer any steady course while accepting that we will always aspire beyond what we can realize. It is hard to put out our hands and touch the past, harder still to bring the past into the future. Nor does the same definition necessarily do from one day to the next. Circumstances transform themselves and our relationship to them. Nothing seems fixed in the world. Familiar ideas don't fit the new reality. The mirror dissolves into a light show. When you watch a light show you see one coloured pattern created by the slides in a projector disintegrating in the very moment in which it appears distinctly and immediately to be altering its relationship to all the other colours which are themselves going through the same process according to their own unique pattern. Revolutionaries now have to accommodate themselves to organizing in the midst of a gigantic three-dimensional light show.[19]

When she wrote those words, the women's movement was just beginning to be heard of in British public life in general. Although the student movements of the late 1960s had been only palely reflected in Britain, there was nevertheless some sense of a 'spirit of 68' still abroad. The miners had demonstrated their power against the Conservative government of Edward Heath in 1972, and although violence in Northern Ireland had escalated, there still seemed to be hope of resolution. The first National Women's Liberation Conference had been held at Ruskin College, Oxford, in 1970, and four main demands had been formulated: equal pay, equal education and job opportunities, free twenty-four-hour nurseries, and free contraception and abortion on demand. Socialist feminists dominated the incipient movement and there was a general atmosphere of enthusiasm and hopefulness.

The climate of energy generated in the early 1970s did not last long, and by the onset of the 1980s the mood was radically different. Sheila Rowbotham's valuable insights and suggestions for future development were submerged in the growing wave of reaction as British society swung to the Right and the Labour movement began to crack under pressure. The old idealism of the early women's movement is not entirely lost and is still prominently present in the women's peace camps around the country, but it comes across as a beleaguered idealism, almost defending its right to exist by restricting the options available. This kind of attitude has led some cynics to question whether the women's movement has not entered into its final agony, whether its time has run out. Some of the women who were publicly involved in the movement a decade ago have moved to the Right, under the guise of being voices of centrist rationality. And at the same time, Britain has fallen into a period of almost undreamed-of economic decline, with unemployment close to four million, and the government beginning to talk about the need for a family policy that will help women feel pride in staying at home and out of the labour market. The picture seems bleak indeed.

The women's movement in Britain in the late 1960s

began in a way reminiscent of the US movement. The disruption of the Miss World competition in London took place in the same year, 1970, as the first National Women's Liberation Conference. The first women's marches on International Women's Day took place in London and in Liverpool in 1971; and small consciousness raising groups mushroomed around the country. At the same time, the new feminist image began to be created. Although mocked in the press as ugly and unfeminine, a substantial number of British feminists chose to wear clothes that were practical and de-emphasized a traditional image of femininity. In Britain probably more than anywhere else, the idea of a feminist uniform became popular, and for a time in the 1970s, dungarees, laced boots and short-cropped hair were every bit as emblematic of a group identity as the old serviceman's tie and blazer. In assuming that new image, feminists were rejecting the other prevailing images of women – the Sex Object, perfumed and provocatively made up for men to ogle, and the Lady, epitomized by Margaret Thatcher in her Marks & Spencer blue suits with crimplene-bowed blouses. Women's theatre groups, like Monstrous Regiment, Beril and the Perils and the Women's Theatre Company, challenged the traditional images of women on stage, deliberately presenting images of androgyny. In addition to the campaigns for equal rights in the workplace and improved child-care conditions, British feminists emphasized the need to alter radically the image of women in society.

The British women's movement grew steadily, in the 1970s, but it grew quietly, with none of the massive street demonstrations that characterized the movements in North America and the rest of Europe. This was perhaps due to the absence of any established British tradition for large-scale public demonstrations, but it was also due to the regional-ization of British feminism. As Michele Barrett points out in *Women's Oppression Today: Problems in Marxist*

Feminist Analysis, the emphasis in the movement has been on the politics of the personal, with its organizational base in small local community groups. She sees this grass-roots base as an important feature of the British women's movement and points out:

Increasingly, women's liberationists have played an important role in attacks on 'the local state', in community struggles over housing, the law, battered women and so on, and this has tended to deflect attention from attempts to influence the state at the level of national policies.[20]

The 'Reclaim the Night' marches were on a tiny scale compared to the European equivalents, but in October 1979, in a massive show of strength, 40,000 people turned out to march in London in protest against the Corrie Bill, the private member's bill that would have revised the liberal 1967 abortion law and made abortion much more difficult to obtain.

The pro-abortion march was organized by the TUC, and the strength of support was undeniable. But the rally also showed the extent of the gap between trade union politics and the women's movement. As the march set off, a group of women staged a protest against being placed fifth in the seven parts of the march, and ran to the front with their banners. Later, in Trafalgar Square, the London Women's Liberation Movement banner was placed by the speakers' platform, and this was then removed by the police. In the ensuing confusion, three women were arrested. At a meeting held at 'A Women's Place', the London women's information centre and meeting place, a statement was issued deploring the arrests and arguing that without the women's liberation movement 'abortion would not have remained a political issue'. There was a feeling that women had been cheated of the chance to protest against abuse of their bodies, and that the TUC position reinforced a sense of powerlessness. Three years later, the 30,000 women who ringed the nuclear-missile base at Greenham Common insisted on the right to protest alone, without male support, carving out for themselves one area of mass separatist action for the first time, and arousing much resentment among men who shared their horrors of the threat of nuclear war.

The Greenham Common all-women protest was clearly an attempt to create a sense of group identity. It was not enough to be opposed to the setting up of American nuclear-missile bases, you had to assert your womanliness as well. In the controversy which followed, the lines of the debate emerged loud and clear. On the one hand, there was the notion that war is essentially a male activity, with the phallus as weapon, an activity which has always been instinctively opposed by women. On the other hand, there was the difficulty of accepting this view, because the logical corollary was that the caring role assigned by male-dominated society to women was their rightful one. Spectres of biological determinism were raised, by men and women alike, and countered by arguments against the large-scale institutionalization of a desire for peace – since the model for such an institutionalizing process is essentially a male one. As Anna Coote and Beatrix Campbell put it:

The channels of democracy in our society – unions, political parties, local councils, Parliament – have been constructed by men, for men. They are not designed to facilitate female participation, and they by-pass important areas of women's lives. They must be forced to change and here, too, men will have to relinquish privilege – the privilege of supreme power. We have grown accustomed to the idea that we are living in a democracy. But we women are still fighting for the franchise. We remain passive in the great blot called 'consensus', which each of the major political parties claims to command. As feminists, we are concerned with disturbing consensus, not with helping to administer it. We will not be the silent majority.[21]

By organizing themselves as an all-women protest, the

Greenham Common protesters saw themselves as fighting on two fronts – against nuclear proliferation and against the structuring of society that relegates women to second place. Significantly, this protest – more than any other – seems to have brought together women from a wide range of classes. It has also united women of all ages and women with very varied political and religious views, and can perhaps be considered the most universal of any of the women's campaigns, a glimpse of post-feminism to come.

The question of what *is* to come in the British women's movement is a troublesome one. In an important pamphlet, *Beyond the Fragments, Feminism and the Making of Socialism*, Sheila Rowbotham, Lynne Segal and Hilary Wainwright argue that socialists have much to learn from the organizational tactics of the women's movement.

The women's movement has made an absolutely vital achievement – or at least the beginnings of it – which no socialist should ignore. It has effectively challenged, on a wide scale, the *self-subordination*, the acceptance of a secondary role, which underpins most forms of oppression and exploitation. This may not be confronting the state – though the women's movement does plenty of that – but unless such a self-subordination is rejected in the minds of men, of the unemployed, of blacks, gays, and all other groups to which socialists aim to give a lead, there will never be much chance of confronting the existing state with a democratic socialist alternative.[22]

Like Margaret Stacey and Marion Price, the authors of *Beyond the Fragments* see the need for organization as a safeguard in dealing with the structures of male-dominated capitalist societies, and when the pamphlet came out many welcomed it with enthusiasm. But a year later, after the Conservative election victory, Elizabeth Wilson, herself a socialist feminist, writing in the *Feminist Review*, spoke the doubts that many feminists had been concealing. In a piece entitled 'Beyond the ghetto: thoughts on *Beyond the Fragments*', she questioned what she called 'the reassuring vision of feminism' that the pamphlet offered to the Left, and called for a reassessment of the link between socialism and feminism. She concluded her article with a series of questions:

Where are we going in the women's movement? What sort of power do we seek? In what way do we wish to make our mark on the world? Do we want a share in the world or do we simply want 'women's sphere' to be given greater value? Or do we want to break out of those dichotomies altogether?[23]

These are questions which have been raised by women in other societies, but which have a particular significance for British feminists because the split between socialist feminism and radical feminism has at times degenerated into a clash between left-wing politics and sexual (i.e. lesbian) politics, an absurd and unfair reduction of two important positions. When we map out the fragmented contours of British feminism, it also becomes clear that the history of organized feminism *is* bound up with the history of middle-class individualism, and the particular grass-roots organization of the British women's movement has links with the history of trade unions, thus making the case even more complex.

In·a later issue of the *Feminist Review*, Val Coultas introduces other disconcerting elements. She points out that the grass-roots women's groups of the early 1970s have steadily declined and that women's demonstrations have become smaller, and she suggests that:

'cultural feminism'; living a 'feminist lifestyle'; reading women's literature, attending women's discos, having women friends has become more of a focus for some women, as an *alternative* to the early campaigning approach of modern feminism.[24]

Most serious of all, she suggests that unlike its US counterpart the women's movement in Britain has not given priority to the campaign for women's rights at work. Stacey and Price discuss the failure of the women's movement to seize formal political power for women, and Val Coultas shows how women have moved away from any mass consensus:

The feminist movement in Britain has tended to concentrate its energies on 'reproductive' struggles – Reclaim the Night demonstrations, pro-abortion campaigns, setting up refuges; the issues have been seen as the main priorities for women. Socialist feminists have also seen it as a particular priority to take up antiracist and anti-imperialist issues such as the struggle of women at Grunwick and the treatment of women in Armagh gaol.

She too would like to see closer affiliation between women's groups and the organized Left. The real enemy of women, she argues, is the capitalist state that maintains women's subjugation in the family; and she insists that reforms can and do benefit women. Greater involvement of women in the public arena would therefore mean a greater impulse towards those reforms which would alleviate the oppression of women trapped in the home, responsible for child care and nursing the aged and the handicapped.

The dilemma for British feminists is a serious one. In the GDR, with the state committed to bringing women out of the home, the context of women's search for identity as individuals within the two collective areas of their own sex and their state is entirely different. British women are still at the beginning of a struggle for basic reforms in the area of domestic labour and childcare, far behind North American and European women in general. Yet there is no guarantee, especially in a time of rising unemployment, crisis in the working-class movement at large, and a government committed to driving women even further away from public life, that they will find much support from socialist men. Moreover, the success of Margaret Thatcher has confirmed the continuance of bourgeois feminism as a powerful element in British life. The hollowness of state encouragement of women was never more clearly exposed than in

1979, when Lady Howe, chairwoman of the Equal Opportunities Commission, resigned in order to devote more time to her husband, who had just been appointed Chancellor of the Exchequer. Women seem likely to have less, not more, influence in the public domain, while losing ground within the family as well.

The picture that emerges of British feminism is both bleak and confused. The supposed progress towards a classless society that was hailed in the 1960s has given way to a society in which class lines are again being rigidly drawn. As the level of unemployment continues to rise and the government preaches the virtues of Victorian values, the place for idealism grows daily more restricted, and in such a context it is difficult to evaluate the impact of the new feminism on British life.

It is perhaps fair to say that the tradition of gradualism that has been such a prominent feature of British political life can also be applied in relation to feminism. One area in which a gradual absorption of new ideas can be traced is women's magazines in the 1970s, when the advent of new feminist publications was matched by changes in the traditional magazines for women. Sandwiched between the more usual features on cookery, knitting, love stories and portraits of the royal family, magazines such as *Woman* and *Woman's Own* have featured articles on alternative child care, lesbianism, abortion, rape and self-help, and have also campaigned for tax reforms and for similar bureaucratic changes.

But both magazines like these and overtly feminist magazines such as *Spare Rib* are part of another strand in the web that entrammels the women's movement in Britain – the tradition of anti-intellectualism that seeks to banish theory and focus attention only on praxis. It is significant that among the many divisions in the women's movement – age v. youth, middle class v. working class, black v. white – there is also the division of intellectual v. non- or anti-intellectual.

The very term 'intellectual' is frequently a derogatory one.

It has often been suggested that intellectuals in British life form a class apart, universally despised by all other levels of the pyramid. In the late 1960s and early 1970s, the equation of intellectualism with left-wing politics and a radical lifestyle accentuated its disparagement in the media. Students were generally depicted as socially undesirable, intellectuals and artists as unnecessary troublemakers, views that have considerably intensified in the past five years. And if there was one appalling lesson to be learned from the Falklands War, it was that the intellectual class in Britain was totally devoid of power, something which had already been apparent in the early 1970s with the escalating crisis in Northern Ireland and the silence from the academics, but that had never been quite so definitively emphasized. With the Left losing ground even in its own working-class power base, and the intellectuals of the country marginalized completely, the position of intellectual feminists has become even more absurd.

Finding myself in that group of middle class, left-wing, intellectual feminists, I was perhaps not unnaturally drawn to the work of another such woman, and was moved by Elizabeth Wilson's autobiographical statement, *Mirror Writing*. 'I did not enter the women's movement in search of an identity,' she says. 'Political activity simply presented itself to me as an imperative and as an escape, a liberation from the privatised obsessions of the search for identity.'[25] And she suggests that women tried to construct a collective identity out of a shared experience of collective oppression, which alas led only to a form of romantic idealism. She argues that there can be no simple reflection of oppression, no precise common core of consensus in the multiplicity of experience. Her book ends with what might be described as another romantic ideal, descending from Mary Wollstonecroft – that the assertion of the individual within the collective identity results in flashes of profound communicative insight. It is a beautifully hopeful vision, but again the context of British feminism poses problems. Perhaps because of the anti-intellectualism in British society, the devaluation of art, and within the arts and academe the profoundly anti-theoretical tradition – whatever the causes – the fact remains that British feminism of the post-1960s period has not resulted in a great flowering of women's culture and of women's theory. In comparison with the proliferation of feminist work by women writers, artists and philosophers throughout Europe, North America and, in increasing numbers, the Third World, very little has emerged in Britain. Many of the prose writers and poets who have been absorbed into the women's movement by readers avid for material have been around for a long time, and several of them could at best be described as anti-feminist. Again, the explanation for this scarcity can be traced back to the polarization of class positions. Having worked for years with Workers' Educational Association creative writing groups, I have had some insight into the extent of the undeveloped creative talent amongst those whom British society excludes from its mainstream and for women the problems are desperately acute. Older women, middle-class women, heterosexual women clinging to the ideas of decorum that are their safeguard in a world of male oppressiveness, can find no outlet for their work. Not long ago, one of the really gifted writers in my group, a tough working-class woman in her fifties who had brought up three children by writing love stories to a formula, began to write short stories and poetry of lucid honesty and good humour which I and the group felt was exceptional. At my recommendation, she sent her material to a women's liberation publication, only to have it returned by the literary editor, an intellectual in her twenties, with a homily on how the writer had patronized the working class. My student returned to writing love stories for her bread and butter and refused to try again to break what she perceived as a barrier set up by well-meaning, politically naive, younger women educated into another class.

In 1971 Germaine Greer wrote *The Female Eunuch*. In this book, long since hailed as a landmark in the literature of women's liberation, she rejects any specific affiliation, and she has often been criticized by other women for refusing to do so. But in her introductory chapter she makes a very significant statement, and one that deserves to be reconsidered at the present time. She defends her book by positing that if it is not ridiculed or reviled it will have failed in its intention:

If the most successful feminine parasites do not find it offensive, then it is innocuous. What they can tolerate is intolerable for a woman with any pride. The opponents of female suffrage lamented that women's emancipation would mean the end of marriage, morality and the state; their extremism was more clear-sighted than the woolly benevolence of liberals and humanists, who thought that giving women a measure of freedom would not upset anything. When we reap the harvest which the unwitting suffragettes sowed we shall see that the anti-feminists were after all right.[26]

Total change in power relations is what Germaine Greer is arguing for, a change so radical that all our assumptions about life and society would be altered. No amount of liberal change, no carefully constructed programme of reform within the limits of our present structures would be adequate – and so we come full circle, to the women's peace movement and to their rejection not only of the structures but also of the values of the society that is proposing to establish nuclear bases in Europe.

The camp at Greenham Common offends public dignity and morality – women have left their families (their rightful place) and gone to live with other like-minded women – *ergo*, they must all be social misfits, lesbians and failures, according to the British press. Yet when we consider the terrifying intricacies of British society, still tied up in knots by its class structures, the mass support elicited by the peace movement is one of the most hopeful signs for the future. The Greenham Common peace camp represents one type of successful women's activity, and cuts across boundaries of class, race and age with great effect. But there has also been another specific example of female militancy in British society of the mid-1980s. During the year-long miners' strike, miners' wives organized themselves into self-help community groups and provided support for their men in ways that defied the conventional stereotype of working-class female submission. The groups of miners' wives organized collections of food and clothing, joined picket lines, travelled around the country to meetings and demonstrations, went abroad to raise money for the strike fund, in short, they became the clearest possible public statement of working-class militancy that had been seen in Britain for many years. And as many of them recognized, once they had been part of such a movement, there could be no going backwards after the strike was over. When the strike finally collapsed early in 1985, the women were bitter but undefeated. They had been tested and had come to understand that they had a role outside the boundaries of the home, a role alongside their men rather than behind them. The impact of the social changes in mining communities created by the work of women during the strike will take a long time to be assessed.

The conflict between socialism and feminism, however, will continue, not only because of the history of this conflict, but also because of the way in which feminism re-emerged in Britain in the 1970s and because of its refusal to look clearly at the conservatism inherent in it. Likewise, the prevailing anti-intellectual climate continues to inhibit the extension of any major theoretical feminist debate, and a leading role in the British feminist movement is still played, as it always was, by women from North America, Australia, Africa and Europe. For example, in a televised discussion on feminists,[27] the traditionally Oxonian views of Mary Warnock were countered by a panel of non-British women, and the programme revealed the absence of any common language.

The women's movement in Britain mirrors rather than counters the problems of changing class consciousness in a period of social and political turmoil. The task of those women who see the fundamentally conservative and philanthropic nineteenth-century tradition of feminist individualism as ideologically undesirable has been made even harder. In the absence of any major theoretical debate, the women's movement has followed the traditions of grassroots socialism and worked in various ways within the community. Not that such work should be disparaged, but the localized nature of women's organizations does point to the enormity of the problems that British women face.

Yet, paradoxically, perhaps, the activities of some British women have come to represent symbols of hope for women's organizations everywhere. The life-enhancing tactics of the women peace campaigners offer a language that people of both sexes can learn to understand. The peace camps function on both the symbolic and the practical level, speaking about women and to women at the same time, and in this respect they differ from other forms of anti-nuclear protest. And the miners' wives' groups came to symbolize working-class mobilization and pride, at a time when the Labour movement appeared to be collapsing in ruins.

The peace women and the miners' wives are, in different ways, the antithesis of Margaret Thatcher. She is a descendant of bourgeois feminism, a woman who has infiltrated male society and striven to occupy a place of power within it. In contrast, both the peace women and the miners' wives have sought to provide an alternative to that vision of society. The task of British feminists in future will lie in understanding the relationship between those opposite visions of women's role, and in building on the base erected by their sisters in the mining communities and the peace camps, even as the strike fades into memory and the makeshift shelters are torn down.

Notes

1 *The Times*, 21 June 1982.

2 R. Strachey, *The Cause: A Short History of the Women's Movement in Great Britain* (London: Virago, 1978), p. 120.

3 A. Coote and B. Campbell, *Sweet Freedom: The Struggle for Women's Liberation* (London: Picador, 1982), p. 107.

4 Equal Opportunities Commission pamphlet, *Short Guide to the Sex Discrimination Act 1975* (London: EOC, 1975).

5 Reproduced in A. Rossi (ed.), *The Feminist Papers* (New York: Bantam, 1973), p. 66.

6 F. Lundberg and M. Farnham, *Modern Woman: The Lost Sex* (New York: Harper & Row, 1947), p. 87.

7 S. Rowbotham, *Women, Resistance and Revolution* (Harmondsworth: Penguin, 1972), p. 45.

8 Quoted in Strachey, *The Cause*, p. 14.

9 Strachey, *The Cause*, p. 14.

10 R. Evans, *The Feminists* (London: Croom Helm, 1977), p. 146.

11 Evans, *Feminists*, pp. 145–6.

12 Evans, *Feminists*, p. 68.

13 Quoted in J. Liddington and J. Norris, *One Hand Tied Behind Us: The Rise of the Women's Suffrage Movement* (London: Virago, 1978), pp. 205–6.

14 Liddington and Norris, *One Hand Tied Behind Us*, p. 210.

15 Evans, *Feminists*, p. 189.

16 V. Woolf, *Women and Writing* (London: Women's Press, 1979), p. 67.

17 M. Stacey and M. Price, *Women, Power & Politics* (London: Tavistock, 1981), p. 92.

18 Stacey and Price, *Women, Power & Politics*, p. 132.

19 S. Rowbotham, *Woman's Consciousness, Man's World* (Harmondsworth: Penguin, 1973), p. 28.

20 M. Barrett, *Women's Oppression Today: Problems in Marxist Feminist Analysis* (London: Verso, 1980), p. 245.

21 Coote and Campbell, *Sweet Freedom*, p. 248.

22 S. Rowbotham, L. Segal and H. Wainwright, *Beyond the Fragments: Feminism and the Making of Socialism* (London: Merlin, 1979), p. 250.

23 E. Wilson, 'Beyond the ghetto: thoughts on *Beyond the Fragments*', *Feminist Review*, no. 4 (1980), pp. 15–28.

24 V. Coultas, 'Feminists must face the future', *Feminist Review*, no. 7 (1981), p. 36.

25 E. Wilson, *Mirror Writing* (London: Virago, 1982), p. 152.

26 G. Greer, *The Female Eunuch* (London: MacGibbon & Kee, 1971), p. 22.

27 *Voices*, Channel 4, 2 March 1983.

Conclusion

In the twenty years since the rebirth of feminism in the 1960s, many changes have taken place. Southern Europe has tended to move to the Left, whilst Britain, West Germany and the United States have moved to the right. The nuclear arms race has accelerated. Student political activity has waned, faded almost into obscure memory. Unemployment has risen drastically, with devastating impact on the hopes of women who had sought to enter the labour market on equal terms with men. Poverty has increased. Creative arts in Western societies are stagnant in comparison with Third World countries. In view of such changes, it is hardly surprising that much of the early dynamism of women's movements seems to have disappeared. And, perhaps most significant of all, in those twenty years a whole new generation of women has emerged, women who have benefited from the years of public focus on the women's movement, but who have none of the idealism of the 1960s generation.

The large-scale campaigns of the late 1960s and early 1970s have died down in the 1980s. The massive abortion rallies, the women picketing the White House and other government offices, the Reclaim the Night marches, the manifestations of women's street theatre, belonged to a particular period and that period ended with the onset of the 1980s. In addition, attempts to organize women nationally have also declined, and large-scale women's conferences have given way to small-scale seminars and workshops.

In place of these public manifestations of a change in women's consciousness, what we have now is more wide-ranging, more subtle and probably more permanent. Changes in employment and facilities for working mothers have been negligible. Rising unemployment in Britain and the United States have shown how precarious the newly won victories for women in the labour market are, and the lack of women in high positions within the professions is a sign of how little progress has been made. The tyranny of women in public office, the Indira Ghandhis and Margaret Thatchers, testifies to no victory at all for women, merely the repetition of the old power-seeking game with new (female) players. And yet, at a time of decreasing employment, with talk of rethinking the whole question of work and leisure in the last two decades of this century, there appear to have been fundamental changes in assumptions about the right of women to work. Linked to these changes have been an alteration in concepts of family, and a re-thinking of the role of fathers and of mothers, as the once-idealized notion of the nuclear family has shown itself to be untenable.

In the four societies discussed in this book, radical change in family structure seem to be under way. These changes are not always linear, not always clearly distin-guished, but they are very definitely happening. In the GDR the gap between the older and younger generations is widening on family issues, as women instigate more and more divorce proceedings, a sign of their growing un-willingness to tolerate bad marriages, and demand abortion as a right. In the United States, more and more men seem to be attempting to understand the meaning of fatherhood as distinct from patriarchy, and the legal system has already begun to acknowledge this trend by awarding custody of children to fathers with increasing frequency. In Italy, the power of the traditional family is being shattered by the new assertiveness of the generation that has created the Red

Brigades and large-scale urban terrorism. Even in Britain, last bastion of conservatism with both a small *c* and a capital *C*, changes are under way. Although the Inland Revenue still writes to husbands about their wives' tax return forms, and although nursery facilities are among the worst in Europe, divorce is on the increase, more women are electing to have their children later in life, more women are prepared to flout conventional anti-child attitudes in order to try to combine motherhood with work.

It is beyond the scope of this book to try to examine in depth the fundamental changes in the concept of the family that are now taking place. Those changes are still so dispersed that it is probably possible to find people in all four societies who would deny that such changes are happening at all. Yet clearly, in spite of the upsurge of moral crusading which tries to argue that only a return to the cane, the hand rocking the cradle, the hangman's noose and the whip will halt a decline into chaos, values are being altered, and a change in the role of women is clearly an intrinsic part of the process.

In discussing families and changes in family structures, any suggestions I put forward will have to be tentative, based more on impressions than on concrete evidence. Those impressions derive from what women are saying, in both art and life, in which there seems to be a chorus of confused voices unified only in their refusal to be slotted into roles defined by men. The rise in divorces initiated by women, the growing number of single-parent families, the demands for abortion and birth control, are all signs of changing consciousness among women, and similar patterns of change are taking place in all the societies discussed in this book.

In contrast to the subtle changes taking place in private, the public organization of women's movements reflects the social context in which they emerge. In consequence, the grass-roots political organization of the British Left has come to be adopted by British women also, whilst in the United States belief in a political system based on the power of the Constitution underlay the whole of the ill-fated ERA campaign, and in Italy the rapid rise and fall of small women's groups mirrors the ever-changing face of Italian political life. In the GDR, organized women's groups reflect the state organization in a like way.

Yet in all four societies, women's concerns are not so far apart, because in none of them as yet has a revaluation of women's culture taken place. In the GDR this process is most advanced, a logical consequence of the drastic improvements in the working conditions of women and the relocation of women in the social hierarchy. East German women writers seem to be saying, 'Thank you very much for putting socialist policies towards women into operation. Now we'll think things out for ourselves and see what we come up with.' Such a demand is much more fundamental and far-reaching than simply asking for state nurseries and equal pay as British and American women still have to do. It marks the start of a search for an alternative cultural base, which perhaps goes some way towards explaining the great success of those few East German women writers whose work is known outside their own language.

Certain problems still remain unsolved. There does not seem to be a valid socio-political explanation of why feminism emerges at certain points in time and then apparently submerges again in various different societies. Since the end of the 1970s, in spite of the growing demand for institutionalized women's courses as part of educational programmes in Western societies, other forms of women's organization are breaking down. Campaigns for nursery facilities are a thing of the past, and nurseries, battered wives' hostels and women's centres have had to struggle for survival on both sides of the Atlantic. Inadequate funding and poor organization have led to the demise of many small-scale women's publications and theatre groups. Larger publishing enterprises have survived through adaptation to the market forces of the existing system, a compromise which, though it may have been necessary, would have been totally unacceptable to the early idealists of the mid-1960s. Even the peace movement, after a triumphant start, has begun to quieten down, with fewer women supporting the mass demonstrations and greater media hostility. In a situation of general economic decline, the best that radical marginal structures can hope for, it seems, is to hold on to a position, the worst is to lose out altogether. What is not happening is the generation of dynamic energy to lead to further achievements.

The idealism and political activism of the late 1960s and early 1970s died out under pressure, just as the idealism of the 1930s had done. For my generation, the loss of that idealism was immense, but for the generations immediately before and after, the picture is very different. For the earlier generation the 1960s ideals were illusory anyway, while for the later generation they are antiquated and unrealistic. Yet the resurgence of the women's movement was closely linked to that 1960s idealism, just as earlier waves of feminism were linked to forms of revolutionary activity. The role of women in the Paris Commune, the rise of feminism together with the rise of socialism right across Europe, and, in an earlier period, the women's groups in revolutionary France testify to a bridge between radical political movements and a form of feminist activity. At times of crisis, women have organized separately alongside the men, a pattern that can be traced back long before the eighteenth century when the term 'feminism' came into being. We have only to think of the role played by women in organising groups to follow Lutheran principles at the beginning of the sixteenth century to see how long standing is the tradition of militant feminist activity.

In *Women, Resistance and Revolution* Sheila Rowbotham

comments that many women in the women's movement are not revolutionaries:

But the demands they make for their own improvement require such a fundamental change in society that they are completely inconceivable without revolution.[1]

This would seem to have been very much the case in any number of revolutionary contexts, but it still leaves certain questions unanswered, of which the most crucial is simply whether feminism can emerge without a revolutionary context that has been set in motion by men and women together. Sheila Rowbotham sees the connection between the oppression of women and colonial and class oppression as a starting-point, and there would seem to be some validity in this view. If we consider the suffrage campaigns of European nations and the United States, the pattern that emerges is one of predominantly middle-class women organizing *for one particular issue*, the right to vote. Once that right was achieved, the organization ceased to exist, because the narrowness of the base could not sustain a more complex structure. This kind of pragmatic feminism can be clearly chartered through the nineteenth and twentieth centuries, and has also been very much in evidence in recent years. But the other feminism, the feminism with a broader socialist base, also subsides with the decline of revolutionary activity in general, and this raises the question of how far feminism comes into being as a reaction to something else, as a mirror to men's radical actions, rather than as an entity in its own right. Looking back to the origins of the term 'feminism', we find that it comes out of a rationalist vision of the world in an age when society was being catalogued differently, and we are still struggling with the terms inherited from that time. Researching this book, I have found the term 'feminism' used in so many different ways that it sometimes seems to have no meaning at all except in the broadest and most generalized sense of 'that which is connected to women organizing themselves'. East German women tend to reject the term completely, whilst nevertheless holding what in other societies could be described as 'feminist' views. Elsewhere others practise a process of selection that restricts use of the same term to a tiny elect minority. I have begun to think that the time may have come to dispense with it altogether, and in coining 'post-feminism' a number of other women appear to be thinking along the same lines. Perhaps the term 'feminism', like rationalism, its not too distant relative, is a term that belongs to an out-dated vision of the world, based on masculinist constructs and ideas, hence the uneasiness surrounding the use of the term today.

Since the onset of organized women's movements in the late 1960s, a good many women have come to question the terminology they use. There has been considerable debate surrounding the term 'feminist', particularly in those countries where language, unlike English, is structured according to gender. At the same time, women have increasingly come to feel uneasy about what was (and often still is) described as feminist activity – the impulse to push women towards proving an abstract equality by competing with men on the same terms as them – by engaging in competition in the labour market, by asserting their public rights to vote and hold office, by demonstrating the capacity of women to hold positions of public power, by trying to prove that there is an equally significant canon of great women writers, artists and thinkers. For some, feminism means just this, as it did to many of the nineteenth-century women; it involves women accepting the framework of the world as it is and proving that they can make their mark on it.

But for others, feminism means something quite different, and involves a process of questioning the fundamentals of Western culture as we know it. It involves asking certain difficult questions, such as why the holding of high public office should be considered more significant than the life lived within the home, why there should be a quest for a female canon of artists and thinkers instead of a challenge to the very concept of the canon itself, why women should want to compete on terms defined by men instead of looking for other alternatives from which to start.

The case against this line of questioning is well known, and has been put strongly by middle-class feminists in particular. If women do not enter the public world, they argue, then that world does not change; if the terms are dictated by men, then the only way that men will understand the flaws in their structuring will be if women prove their ability to compete and then suggest alternatives at a later stage; if the established criteria of greatness and social importance are called into doubt, then order and practicality will be replaced by anarchy and inconsistency. It is comforting to be able to describe someone as a 'great politician' or a 'great writer', and disquieting to begin questioning the basis of such assumptions of greatness. In the pragmatic United States, the arguments for publicly acclaimed feminism seem to have won the day, and women do compete openly with men, following the advice their nineteenth-century sisters would have given. In Italy, as in France and West Germany, where 'post-feminism' has been in use for several years now, there is a much greater sense of uneasiness about the absorption of women into existing structures, and in the GDR all such questions as those above are posed from a completely different perspective. Perhaps only in Britain is the extent of the complexity of these questions being revealed, as trends in European and North American feminism are filtered by traditional British concepts of feminism and by the contribution of the British socialist tradition.

The term 'feminist' may be unclear and may be used by the media as a stick with which to beat women who challenge the established order in any way, it may have become as loaded a word as 'suffragette' once was; never-theless it has come to acquire international recognition of a kind. The term has entered the daily vocabulary of people across the world, and with it have come a whole range of terms that were not previously in common use. 'Sexism', something that I never encountered until my late teens, is an issue even for very young children. My daughters have grown up with the notion of sexism, as have their class-mates, and have developed an ability to perceive not only explicit sexist attitudes but implicit ones as well, sometimes more acutely than I can. These slight linguistic changes mark much more significant changes in attitude, and it is hard to imagine how the present generation of ten-year-olds will accept a philosophy, already outdated when I was a child, that presents the proper place of women as being firmly within the home. It may be harder nowadays for social injustice to be clearly seen, since in the First World the poor do not feature as prominently in our daily lives as they did in the 1930s, for example, but paradoxically it has become easier to perceive sexist prejudices in operation.

The far-reaching effects of this, at present miniscule, change can only be imagined, but it does seem that already, before feminism as such reappeared in the late 1960s, massive changes in the pattern of family life were under way. Divorce, much more than abortion, changes social structures on a large scale, and the proportion of women petitioning for divorce in eastern and western Europe and in North America testifies to the growing unwillingness of women to settle for inadequate relationships, even if the price is complete upheaval within the family. Women had begun to dismantle the traditional family structures even before they had the terminology of feminism to fall back on, and this process of change has in no way declined; rather the opposite can be seen from divorce statistics in any number of countries.

Changes in terminology, useful though they may be, are

not the principle gain from the latest upsurge of feminist activity. The major step forward has been in the debates about the existence of a separate women's culture, emerging from a rethinking of the definitions of men and women. Simone de Beauvoir introduced the idea of woman as the Other, the being 'defined and differentiated with reference to man and not he with reference to her',[2] and another generation of women has begun to explore the meaning of that Otherness. The western European explorations of the alienation of women from the daily (male) language they use, the work of East German women writers, the thrashing out of ideas of women's history and mythology that has been going on in the United States, all these activities go far beyond the kind of writing that simply exposes the deprived state of women in the world. Together with other women, I have come to look again at all kinds of assumptions that I previously held with confidence. I have come to look again, for example, at the idea of separate yet coexistent and equal male and female cultures, at the system in some parts of the world, deemed 'primitive' in comparison with Western cultures, in which men and women occupy separate houses and have clearly separate activities to which no evaluative status is given. Looking outwards from the complacent presumptions of Western middle-class society involves both reassessment of other cultures and reassessment of one's own culture in previous stages. Following the impulse of French and Italian women of my generation, I have come to reconsider the significance of the convents as centres of learning, as refuges for women in the Middle Ages rather than as places of incarceration, and have begun to recognize the distortions of our sense of own history that derive from judging the past with the ideal of rationalism as our strongest criterion. We have accepted unquestioningly the post-rationalist view that society has been improving steadily for the past three centuries, since the beginning of industrialization. If we rethink that assumption, all kinds of alternatives come to light. Those activities which have so frequently been derided as marginal and womanly, activities such as embroidery, knitting, china painting, cooking and similar domestic jobs, can be restored to their proper status once we overthrow the criteria set up in the eighteenth century. All those activities occupied a place of importance in pre-industrialized society that is only just beginning to be recognized.

What we are experiencing is a process of re-evaluation, not only of the roles performed by women in the creation of cultures, but of the whole system of classifying and cataloguing culture. The attempt to rediscover the contribution of women to history is only the tip of the iceberg; of much further reaching significance is the exploration of how the history of culture comes to be written, and why, in that writing, women have been downgraded, marginalized, frequently ignored. I feel strongly that it is far too simple to think of the Enlightenment as the period that marked the beginning of modern civilization; there is a case to be answered that the supposed light of knowledge and scientific achievement in fact plunged Western civilization (and especially women) into greater darkness. Far from marking improvements in the living and working conditions of women, the eighteenth century marked the start of the exclusion of women from education, from the professions and from the power invested in property, in ways that would have been unthinkable during the Renaissance, and the start of an age in which women of the middle classes were confined uselessly to their homes, to be waited on by working-class women whose sisters were employed in the mines and factories together with their hordes of young children. When at the end of the nineteenth century William Morris's Utopian socialist vision led him to rethink what life had signified in the Middle Ages, he was showing his own (male) awareness of the ravages wrought by the post-Enlightenment ideology of a social structure based on reason.

Probably the greatest gain from the past twenty or so years of development in social awareness of the changing function of women has been a sense of continuity and connection that crosses (albeit with difficulty) barriers of class, race and nationality, linking women through their sexuality. I am amazed to think that for so long I could seriously have imagined that I could understand the minds of men or have them understand my thought processes; whatever understanding and communication exists between men and women starts from differences in experience rather from sameness of experience. Working at the same factory bench, achieving the same exam results, sharing the same bed, does not cancel the fundamental differences between men and women. And just as inherent differences signal separateness of the sexes, so inherent similarities signal connections within single-sex groups, despite the existence of other sets of barriers. The force that unites women from various cultures is therefore not so much a commonality of oppression suffered, and is certainly not any coherent ideological stance; it is, rather, the way in which the biological is reconciled with the social. For some women, as for some men, this process of attempting reconciliation has been destructive, for others it has proved impossible, but nevertheless it underscores all the theoretical debates about sexual difference. There have been many attempts to prove the biological inferiority of women, and recently women have turned those reactionary arguments on their heads, suggesting that biological difference need not be evaluated from a standpoint determined by a male-dominated society. Unquestionably, women move differently through space and time, with the menstrual clock mechanism built into their systems, but it is absurd to assume that such differences might also mean that women do not have equal intellectual and creative capacities. As I write this page, the child that will be born in the next two or three weeks is kicking me with all the energy of someone who is eager to come out and start to sample what life has to offer. My experience of carrying a child and giving birth is shared by millions of women, shared by no man ever, and yet remains uniquely mine. This recognition of one's perception of the world as something at once unique, shared and different is the principal lesson I have learned from being part of the process of changing consciousness of women of my generation. The final result of a process of comparison is never likely to be the clarification of absolutes, but rather perception of the greater complexity of the web of problems that surround each individual and a recognition by the individual of where she stands in the web.

Notes

1 S. Rowbotham, *Women, Resistance and Revolution* (London: Penguin, 1972), p. 246.
2 S. de Beauvoir, *The Second Sex* (Harmondsworth: Penguin, 1977), p. 16.

Select Bibliography

The proliferation of books and articles on women over the past two decades makes it virtually impossible for any bibliography to be exhaustive. In this selection of books for further reading, I have listed those texts which I found personally to be of use and interest, together with some which contain excellent, more extensive bibliographies.

I have tried, wherever possible, to supply details of texts in English. In the Italian section, however, this has proved almost impossible, so a certain number of key texts are given in the original language.

The United States

Altbach, E. H. (ed.), *From Feminism to Liberation* (Cambridge, Mass.: Schenkman, 1971).

Atkinson, T.-G., *Amazon Odyssey* (New York: Links, 1974).

Beard, M., *Women as Force in History* (New York: Collier Macmillan, 1946).

Brown, D., *Women of the Wild West* (London and Sydney: Pan, 1975 [1958]). First published in Great Britain as *The Gentle Tamers* (London: Barrie & Jenkins, 1973).

Cardew, M. L., *The New Feminist Movement* (New York: Russell Sage Foundation, 1974).

Cott, N. F. and Pluck, E. H., *A Heritage of Her Own: Toward a New Social History of American Women* (New York: Simon & Schuster, 1979).

Daly, M., *Beyond God the Father: Toward a Philosophy of Women's Liberation* (Boston: Beacon, 1973).

Daly, M., *The Church and the Second Sex* (New York: Harper & Row, 1975).

Daly, M., *Gyn/Ecology* (London: Women's Press, 1979).

Daly, M., *Pure Lust: Elemental Feminist Philosophy* (New York: Beacon, 1985).

Douglas, A., *The Feminization of American Culture* (New York: Alfred Knopf, 1978).

Eisenstein, Z., *The Radical Future of Liberal Feminism* (New York and London: Longman, 1981).

Firestone, S., *The Dialectic of Sex* (London: Cape, 1971).

Friedan, B., *The Feminine Mystique* (New York: Dell, 1963).

Friedan, B., *The Second Stage* (New York: Summit, 1981).

Fuller, M., *Woman in the Nineteenth Century* (New York: Norton, 1971).

Goldman, E., *Living My Life* (New York: New American Library, 1977).

Gordon, L., *Woman's Body, Woman's Right: A Social History of Birth Control in America* (New York: Penguin, 1977).

Gornick, V., and Moran, B. (eds), *Woman in Sexist Society: Studies in Power and Powerlessness* (New York: New American Library, 1971).

Hole, J. and Levine, E., *Rebirth of Feminism* (New York: Quadrangle, 1971).

Kessler-Harris, A., *Out to Work: A History of Wage-Earning Women in the United States* (New York: Oxford University Press, 1982).

Kraditor, A. S., *The Ideas of the Woman Suffrage Movement, 1890–1920* (New York: Doubleday, 1971).

Lerner, G. (ed.), *The Female Experience: An American Documentary* (Indianapolis, Ind.: Bobbs-Merrill, 1977).

Marlow, H. C. and Davis, H. M., *The American Search for Woman* (Santa Barbara, Calif. and Oxford: Clio, 1976).

Millett, K., *Sexual Politics* (New York: Doubleday, 1970).

Morgan, R., *Sisterhood is Powerful* (New York: Vintage Books, 1970).

Olsen, T., *Silences* (London: Virago, 1980).

Rendall, J., *The Origins of Modern Feminism: Women in Britain, France and the United States 1780–1860* (London: Macmillan, 1985).

Rich, A., *Of Woman Born: Motherhood as Experience and Institution* (London: Virago, 1977).

Rogin, Lerch and Hartsock (eds), *Building Feminist Theory. Three Years of the Best of Quest* (New York and London: Longman, 1981).

Rosenberg, R., *Separate Spheres: Intellectual Roots of Modern Feminism* (New Haven, Conn.: Yale University Press, 1982).

Rossi, A. (ed.), *The Feminist Papers* (New York: Bantam, 1973).

Roszak, B. and Roszak, T., *Masculine/Feminine: Readings in Sexual Mythology and the Liberation of Women* (New York: Harper & Row, 1969).

Ryan, M. P., *Womanhood in America: From Colonial Times to the Present* (New York: New Viewpoints, 1975).

Scott, A. F. (ed.), *Women in American Life* (Boston: Houghton Mifflin, 1970).

Scott, A. F. (ed.), *The American Woman: Who Was She?* (Englewood Cliffs, NJ: Prentice-Hall, 1971).

Stanton, E. C., *Eighty Years and More* (New York: Schocken, 1971).

Vetterling-Braggin, M., Elliston, F. A. and English, J. (eds), *Feminism and Philosophy* (Totowa, NJ: Rowman & Littlefield, 1977).

Ware, S., *Beyond Suffrage: Women in the New Deal* (Cambridge, Mass. and London: Harvard University Press, 1981).

The German Democratic Republic

Allendorf, M. *et al.*, *Women in the GDR* (Dresden: Verlag Zeit im Bild, 1978).

Anderson, E. (ed.), *Blitz aus Heitern Himmel* (Rostock: VEB Hinstorff, 1975).

Bebel, A., *Woman under Socialism* (New York: Schocken, 1971).

Boxer, M. and Quataert, J. (eds), *Socialist Women: European Socialist Feminism in the 19th and early 20th Century* (New York: Elsevier, 1978).

Dennis, M., 'Women and work in the GDR' in I. Wallace (ed.), *The GDR Under Honecker, 1971–1981, GDR Monitor* Special Series no. 1 (Dundee, 1981).

Dworkin, A., *Right Wing Women* (London: Women's Press, 1983).

Einhorn, B., 'Socialist emancipation: the women's movement in the German Democratic Republic', *Women's Studies International Quarterly* vol. 4, no. 4, (1981), pp. 435–52.

Evans, R., *The Feminists* (London: Croom Helm, 1977).

Feyl, R., *Der Lautlose Aufbruch* (Berlin: Neues Leben, 1981).

Heitlinger, A., *Women and State Socialism* (London: Macmillan, 1979).

Königsdorf, H., *Meine Ungehörigen Träume* (Berlin: Aufbau-Verlag, 1978).

Kuhrig, H. and Speigner, W., *Wie Emanzipiert sind die Frauen in der DDR?* (Cologne: Pahl Rugenstein, 1979).

Macpherson, K., 'Christa Wolf in Edinburgh. An interview', *GDR Monitor* no. 1 (Dundee, 1979), pp. 1–12.

Macpherson, K., 'In search of new prose: Christa Wolf's reflections on writing and the writer in the 1960s and 1970s', *New German Studies*, vol. 9, no. 1 (Hull, Spring, 1981), pp. 1–13.

Macpherson, K., 'Christa Wolf's prose and essay work of the 1960s', in G. Bartram and T. Waine (eds), *Culture and Society in the GDR*, *GDR Monitor*, Special Series no. 2 (Dundee, 1984).

Macpherson, K., 'Christa Wolf's *Kindheitsmuster*', in I. Wallace (ed.), *The Writer and Society in the GDR* (Tayport: Hutton, 1984), pp. 103–19.

Mallinckrodt, A., *Research on the GDR 'auf Englisch'* (Washington, DC: Missourian, 1984).

Menschik, J. and Leopold, E., *Gretchens Rote Schwestern: Frauen in der DDR* (Frankfurt am Main: Fischer Taschenbuchverlag, 1974).

Morgner, I., *Leben und Abentener der Trobadora Beatriz nach Zeugnissen ihner Spielfrau Laura* (Berlin: Aufbau-Verlag, 1974).

Morgner, I., *Life and Adventures of Trobadora Beatriz as Chronicled by her Minstrel Laura*, trans. with introduction by F. Achberger (Fall, Wash.: New German Critique, 1978).

Morgner, I., *Amanda: Ein Hexenroman* (Berlin: Aufbau-Verlag, 1983).

Pore, R., *A Conflict of Interest: Women in German Social Democracy, 1919–1933* (Westport, Conn.: Greenwood, 1981).

Quataert, J., 'Unequal partners in an uneasy alliance: women and the working class in imperial Germany', in M. Boxer and J. Quataert (eds), *Socialist Women: European Socialist Feminism in the 19th and Early 20th Century* (New York: Elsevier, 1978), pp. 112–45.

Scott, H., *Women and Socialism: Experiences from Eastern Europe* (London: Alison & Busby, 1976).

Shaffer, H. J., *Women in the Two Germanies* (Oxford: Pergamon, 1981).

Stephenson, J., *The Nazi Organization of Women* (London: Croom Helm, 1975).

Thönnessen, W., *The Emancipation of Women: The Rise and Decline of the Women's Movement in German Social Democracy, 1863–1933* (London: Pluto Press, 1973).

Wander, M., *Guten Morgen, du Schöne* (Berlin: Aufbau-Verlag, 1977).

Wander, M., *Tagebücher und Briefe* (Berlin: Aufbau-Verlag, 1981).

Wolf, C., *The Quest for Christa T.* (London: Hutchinson, 1971).

Wolf, C., *The Reader and the Writer* (Berlin: Seven Seas, 1977).

Wolf, C., *A Model Childhood* (New York: Farrar, Strauss & Giroux, 1980).

Wolf, C., *No Place on Earth* (London: Virago, 1983).

Wolf, C., *Cassandra* (London: Virago, 1984).

See also:

Neue Deutsche Literatur (1086 Berlin, Friedrichstrasse 16/170, PF 1299, GDR).

GDR Bulletin (Department of Germanic Languages, Box 1104, Washington University, St. Louis, Miss. 63130).

GDR Monitor (1 Richmond Terrace, Dundee DD2, 1BQ).

GDR Review (Verlag Zeit im Bild, Julian-Griman-Allee, 801 Dresden, GDR).

Studies in GDR Culture and Society (Department of German and Russian, Bowling Green State University, Bowling Green, Ohio 43403).

Statistical publications of Panorama DDR, Berlin, especially:
Families in the GDR (1983).
Women and Socialism (1983).

Italy

Caldwell, L., 'Abortion in Italy', *Feminist Review*, no. 7 (1981), pp. 49–64.

Caprioli, A. and Vaccaro, L., *La donna nella Chiesa, oggi* (Turin: Elle Di Ci, 1981).

Cutrufelli, M. R., *L'invenzione della donna: Miti e tecniche dello sfruttamento* (Milan: Mazzotta, 1974).

Del Miglio, C. and Fedeli, L., *Il problema donna* (Rome: Città Nuova, 1980).

Fedeli, L., *Mondo 3 femminile: Crisi d'identità e scienza della donna* (Rome: Bulzoni, 1982).

Fraire, M., *Lessico politico delle donne: Cinema, letteratura, arti visive* (Milan: Gulliver, 1979).

La Vigna, C., 'The marxist ambivalence toward women: between socialism and feminism in the Italian socialist party', in M. Boxer and J. Quataert (eds), *Socialist Women: European Socialist Feminism in the 19th and Early 20th Century* (New York: Elsevier, 1978), pp. 146–81.

Lemoine-Luccioni, E., *Il taglio femminile* (Rome: Edizioni delle Donne, 1976).

Macciocchi, M. A., *La donna nera: La donna e la traversata del fascismo* (Milan: Feltrinelli, 1976).

Macciocchi, M. A., *Sessualità femminile e fascismo* (Milan: Feltrinelli, 1977).

Macciocchi, M. A., *Le donne e i loro padroni* (Milan: Mondadori, 1980).

Macciocchi, M. A., *Duemila anni di felicità* (Milan: Mondadori, 1983).

Mizzau, M., *Eco e Narciso, parole e silenzi nel conflitto uomo–donna* (Turin: Boringhieri, 1979).

Pomata, G., *La scienza è coscienza: donne e potere nella società borghese* (Bologna: La Nuova Italia, 1979).

Rasy, E., *La lingua della nutrice: Percorsi e tracce dell'espressione femminile* (Rome: Edizioni delle Donne, 1978).

Ravaioli, C., *La questione femminile: Intervista col PCI* (Milan: Bompiani, 1976).

Rossanda, R., *Le altre: Conversazioni a Radiotre sui rapporti tra donne e politica, libertà, fraternità, ugualianza, democrazia, fascismo, resistenza, stato, partito, rivoluzione, femminismo* (Milan: Bompiani, 1979).

Rossi, R., *Le parole delle donne* (Rome: Riuniti, 1978).

Scroppo, E., *Donne, privato e politico: storie personali di 21 donne del PCI* (Milan: Mazzotta, 1979).

Seroni, A., *La questione femminile in Italia 1970–1977* (Rome: Riuniti, 1977).

Spagnoletti, R., *I movimenti femministi in Italia: le posizione teorico-politiche del femminismo italiano dalle origini in un'antologia dei documenti più significativi (1966–71)* (Rome: Savelli, 1978).

Teodori, M. A., *Contro l'aborto di classe* (Rome: Savelli, 1975).

Tornabuoni, L. and Reggiani, S., *Sorelle d'Italia: l'immagine della donna dal '68 al '78* (Milan: Bompiani, 1978).

Britain

Barrett, M., *Women's Oppression Today: Problems in Marxist Feminist Analysis* (London: Verso, 1980).

Beddoe, D., *Discovering Women's History* (London: Pandora, 1983).

Branca, P., *Silent Sisterhood: Middle-Class Women in the Victorian Home* (London: Croom Helm, 1975).

Brunt, R. and Rowan, C., *Feminism, Culture and Politics* (London: Lawrence & Wishart, 1982).

Coote, A. and Campbell, B., *Sweet Freedom: The Struggle for Women's Liberation* (London: Picador, 1982).

Coward, R., *Patriarchal Precedents* (London: Routledge & Kegan Paul, 1983).

Davies, M. L., *Maternity: Letters from Working Women* (London: Virago, 1978).

Greer, G., *The Female Eunuch* (London: MacGibbon & Kee, 1971).

Greer, G., *The Obstacle Race* (London: Secker & Warburg, 1979).

Hamilton, R., *The Liberation of Women* (London: Allen & Unwin, 1978).

Liddington, J. and Norris J., *One Hand Tied Behind Us: The Rise of the Women's Suffrage Movement* (London: Virago, 1978).

McCrindle, J. and Rowbotham, S., *Dutiful Daughters: Women Talk about their Lives* (Harmondsworth: Penguin, 1979).

Mitchell, J., *Woman's Estate* (Harmondsworth: Penguin 1971).

Pankhurst, S., *The Suffragette Movement* (London: Virago, 1977).

Ramelson, M., *Petticoat Rebellion* (London: Lawrence & Wishart, 1967).

Rowbotham, S., *Women, Resistance and Revolution* (London: Penguin, 1972).

Rowbotham, S., *Hidden from History: 300 Years of Women's Oppression and the Fight Against it* (London: Pluto, 1973).

Rowbotham, S., *Dreams and Dilemmas* (London: Virago, 1983).

Rowbotham, S., Segal, L. and Wainwright, H., *Beyond the Fragments: Feminism and the Making of Socialism* (London: Merlin, 1979).

Spender, D., *Invisible Women: The Schooling Scandal* (London: Writers & Readers Publishing Coop., 1982).

Stacey, M. and Price, M., *Women, Power & Politics* (London: Tavistock, 1981).

Strachey, R., *The Cause: A Short History of the Women's Movement in Great Britain* (London: Virago, 1978).

Weeks, G., *Sex, Politics and Society* (London: Longman, 1981).

Wilson, E., *Women and the Welfare State* (London: Tavistock, 1977).

Wilson, E., *Only Halfway to Paradise: Women in Postwar Britain, 1945–1968* (London: Tavistock, 1980).

Wilson, E., *Mirror Writing* (London, Virago, 1982).

Wilson, E., *No Turning Back* (London, Virago, 1982).

Woolf, V., *Women and Writing* (London: Women's Press, 1979).

See also:

Feminist Review (11 Carleton Gardens, Brecknock Road, London N19, 5AQ).

M/F (69 Randolph Road, London W9 1DW; from 1978).

Index